THE WEEKEND GARDENER

THE

Henry Agg

WEEKEND

Weekend projects & everyday inspiration for the busy gardener

GARDENER

Contents

Welcome to weekend gardening 6

PLAN

Planning for a project 10
Environmental factors 12
The practicalities 18
The legalities 20
Instinctive design 24
Your budget 26
Managing your time 28

BUILD

Ready to go 36
Essential tools 38
Concrete and mortar 42
Boundaries 46
Project: How to install a slatted fence 48
Patios and paths 52
Project: How to lay a patio 58
Project: How to lay a rustic brick path 68
Steps 73
Project: How to build block and brick steps 74
Retaining and garden walls 80
Project: How to build a retaining wall 82
Beds and borders 88
Project: How to build a raised bed 90
Outdoor structures 93
Project: How to build a pergola 94
Outdoor seating 98
Lighting 100
Water features 102
Project: How to build a sunken water feature 104
Plant supports 108
Project: How to build a hazel lattice 110
Compost 114
Project: How to build a compost bay 116

PLANT

Planting design principles 120

Planting styles 128

Choosing your plants 130

My favorite plants 132

Right plant, right place 134

Project: How to plant a hedge 138

Project: How to plant a tree 142

Project: How to plant bare-root roses 146

Project: How to plant herbaceous perennials 148

Project: How to plant bulbs 150

Project: How to lay sod 152

Plants for free 154

MAINTAIN

Yearly maintenance 162

Spring tasks 166

Summer tasks 172

Fall tasks 176

Winter tasks 182

Resources 186

Index 187

Acknowledgments 191

Welcome to weekend gardening

I'm convinced that anyone can build a beautiful garden if they put their mind to it. You don't need qualifications, years of experience, or even lots of time—you just need some determination and free weekends!

How hard can it be? Little did I know that this very question would define the next significant chapter of my life. When we bought our first home, I remember venturing into the garden the moment we got the keys and thinking to myself, "This has potential."

Given that I had no professional gardening or landscaping experience, I contacted some local landscapers to quote for what was a fairly basic plan—a patio, lawn, and some very simple borders. I was gobsmacked by the quotes I received, a seemingly extortionate amount of money for two weeks' work. That is when my gardening and landscaping journey began.

I decided to teach myself how to do the fundamentals of landscaping by reading books, watching YouTube videos, and learning from my mistakes along the way. From there, I managed to design and complete my first two landscaping projects with no professional help, all while working full-time in my corporate role Monday to Friday and making the most of my spare time on the weekends.

At that stage, I had no landscape design or horticultural qualifications. Everything I did was what I call instinctive design: observing the space, getting a feel for what would work in different areas, and then getting to work. To this day, having designed two of my own gardens and many more for clients, I still feel some of the best gardens are created by instinct, not by perfectly manicuring the space sitting next to a drawing board or behind a computer.

Before I started, I had no idea how much gardening would benefit my well-being. Tackling the garden projects myself was a massive distraction from the everyday stresses I felt in the corporate world. I found that every time I went outside and connected with nature, my mind was put at ease and everything else became irrelevant during that moment.

As someone who started out with no professional gardening or landscaping skills, I would have loved to have been able to turn to one book that highlighted everything I needed to know on planning, building, and planting a garden. So my intention with this book is to take everything I learned along the way and package that up as an easily digestible read so you can tackle your very own project. It's a practical guide to building a beautiful space, managing time and cost, while nurturing your mind and body throughout the process.

The sense of satisfaction and reward from creating your own garden is immense. Not only will you save yourself thousands of dollars, but also you can proudly sit outside and tell people, "I did this." It's a beautiful feeling, so let's get started.

Plan

What does your yard mean to you and how do you want it to function? Are you looking to create a tranquil space to break away from the hustle and bustle of working life? Do you want a functional space to entertain guests and family all year round? Or perhaps you'd like a place to grow your own fresh fruit and vegetables. This is where I always start when I'm planning a new garden or making adjustments to an existing space: define the purpose and then create the vision.

This chapter will walk you through the planning stage, what you should consider, how to create a plan, and then how to execute your plan in a methodical way.

Planning for a project

If you have picked up this book to make some changes to your landscaping, such as adding a new border or a raised bed for growing veggies, or even if you plan to redesign the entire space, you've come to the right place! Many of the projects in this book can be completed in one or two weekends. First, though, you need to understand your yard and how it works before you can get going. Then you can formulate your vision for the space.

Starting a new gardening project or planning a complete redesign is exciting, but if you're tackling the project solo without the help of any professionals, it can also be a daunting prospect. That is certainly how I felt at the beginning. Let me reassure you: you can achieve fantastic results with a good plan, some determination, and a willingness to step out of your comfort zone and try new things. I would say simply commit to the process, put everything into it, and give it a try. Let's have a look at what you need to consider before you start.

I find it's a good idea to make notes about existing plants, views, aspect, and materials that could be reused (like the obelisk) as I walk around the space.

Understanding your space

First, you need to understand how your space works and functions. Often, you soon realize that there are very good reasons for certain features, shrubs, or trees being positioned where they are. For example, you may not like a particular tree in the yard, but it could be acting as a windbreak from prevailing wind, which you discover only during windier times of the year.

Knowing your yard before you start a project also allows you to understand the environmental factors. Take note of the following so you have a dossier to refer back to when designing and building:

- Your soil type and its pH, so you can select plants that are suited to your conditions (see pp.12–13).
- Drainage (see p.14) may impact where you plan to have a seating area or patio, or affect an existing one—for instance, if the yard is prone to flooding.
- Your yard's aspect (see pp.14–15) will dictate where you build terraces, seating areas, or the planting you can have.
- Microclimates (see p.16) will have an influence on planting and the positioning of key features.
- Your yard's topography (see pp.16–17) may need to be factored into a building or planting project.
- You may find there are particular routes you always walk and that you create your own "lines of desire." Well-worn walkways often tell the story of someone getting from A to B in the quickest possible way, and these routes can feed into your landscaping plan.

Brand-new landscaping

If you have just moved into a new home and you've picked up this book for inspiration, I would advise you to just live with your yard for six months to a year before embarking on your new venture. You won't know what plants already exist. If you've moved into a new house in winter, for instance, and start making plans immediately, you could be digging up lots of hidden gems, so it's worth waiting to see what starts coming up in spring and summer.

Goals and aspirations

Once you have a clear understanding of your space, you need to define your goals and vision for the landscaping to ensure you set off on the right foot. Then you can start to plan and build landscaping that fits your brief.

For example, you may want a very practical, open space that is low maintenance because you only get a few hours to spend in it over the weekend. In this scenario, your choice of hard landscaping materials and planting will be dictated by that goal. Perhaps your goal is to focus on just a few projects, such as ripping up decking and laying a patio, or increasing the size of planting areas.

You may live by yourself and have your own yard, in which case, you have only your own goals and aspirations to consider. Or you may have a partner, and children running around, and perhaps a pet. If you live with others, it's important to come up with a collective goal and vision—after all, the yard will be a shared space and you want it to cater for everyone's needs, including any resident pets.

As well as how you would like the space to function, think about the overall aesthetic. Create mood boards from inspirational content online and start to write down notes on how you want your yard to look. Write this down on paper or, if you're feeling creative, build an online presentation with all of your mood boards and inspirational content in one place. It will be a great dossier to refer back to and will ensure you are continuously aligning with your goal and vision for the space.

Environmental factors

Environmental conditions play a vital part in creating a sustainable and thriving outdoor space, so it's important to understand your yard's environment in the planning stages. Once you have your vision nailed down and you know what your guiding North Star is, assess your yard's environmental conditions before you get started with any of the works.

Know your soil

It's essential to understand your soil pH and soil type, because they give you a great indication of your yard's specific growing conditions and what you can and can't do with planting.

Soil pH

The pH of soil refers to how alkaline or acidic it is: acidic soil has a pH of less than 7, and alkaline soil has a pH above 7. A pH of 6.5 is the best of both worlds: a loamy, neutral soil in which you can grow most plants.

Finding out your soil pH gives you an indication of what plants will thrive in your yard and what you should avoid. Some plants, such as lilacs, prefer slightly alkaline soils, and others, such as rhododendrons, more neutral or acidic soil. Refer to p.136 for my recommendations for acid- and alkaline-loving plants.

You can test soil pH using a store-bought testing kit, which consists of test tubes and a solution, or a soil-testing probe that you stick into the ground in various different places around the yard to take pH and moisture readings.

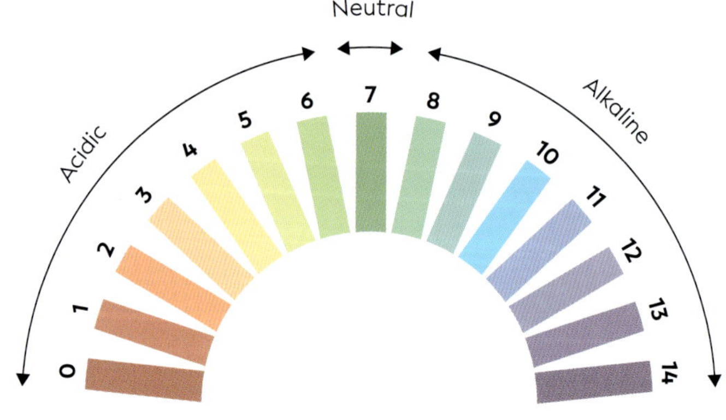

Acidic, neutral, and alkaline soils
Soil can have a pH that ranges from very acidic to very alkaline, with most soils falling somewhere in between. A soil pH of 7 is neutral.

Soil type

The overall makeup and structure of soil is referred to as the soil type. It's determined by the individual sand, silt, and clay particles the soil contains. Typically, there are four types of soil that you might find in your yard: clay, sandy, loam, and silt. They each have differing properties and provide unique growing conditions for plants.

Your soil type will have an impact on planting and drainage. You may find that you have chalk underneath your topsoil, as I have, which means you need to mulch it to add a good depth of organic matter, improving drainage and soil fertility, especially if it hasn't been cultivated before. Peat is unlikely to be in your yard and shouldn't be dug.

Testing your soil type

To test your soil, dig pilot holes and lift out a sample section. Roll the soil sample in your hands.

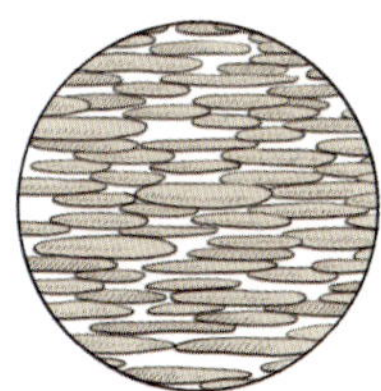

Clay If the sample clumps together and you can roll it up like a sausage, you have predominantly clay soil. It may have a shiny appearance.

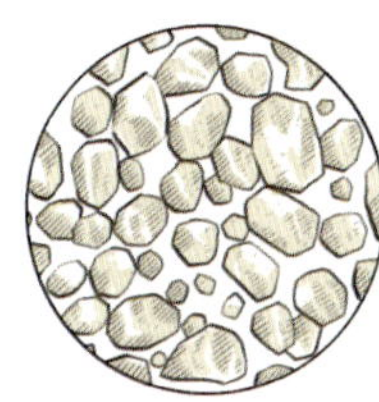

Sand If the sample crumbles to a fine dust and has a gritty texture, you have a more sandy soil.

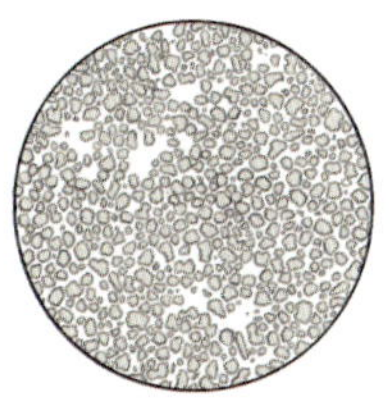

Silt If the sample does not hold its shape and has a slippery texture, you have a silty soil.

Loam If the sample clumps together but doesn't hold its shape, you have a more loamy soil, which is an almost even split of clay, sand, and silt particles, making it the perfect growing medium for plants to thrive.

Drainage

Drainage is an area to explore and understand before you get started. If you have drainage issues, such as flooding on your existing patio area or green spaces, then now is the time to plan to improve it with relevant drainage systems and factor this into the new landscaping. After all, you wouldn't want to build a beautiful, new oasis and then see all of your hard work flooded in heavy rainfall.

Look for signs of damp or boggy areas in your soil and any lawn areas to determine if the yard is prone to waterlogging during wetter months. If there are no obvious damp areas, you can dig pilot holes and see what's going on beneath the soil surface compared to other areas.

You will also need to understand where any surface water from patios or paths is being directed to currently; this may be the same solution you use for the new design.

You may have a an underground drainage system that absorbs rainwater in the yard. Knowing about this before you start building will be extremely helpful because you may wish to direct any surface water from new patios and paths into the existing drainage system. You can pay for a separate utilities search of your property, or it may be detailed on your title deeds.

One thing to consider is where your waterproofing is on your house or any adjoining buildings, as this will often impact the finished height of your patios and paths (see p.61). It's often indicated by a layer of black between the mortar joints.

Your yard's aspect

Another key element you need to understand is your yard's orientation or aspect. Is it north, east, south, or west facing? You can find this out using a compass on your phone.

Your yard's aspect determines how much sunlight and shade you are likely to experience as the sun moves across the sky. For example, a north-facing yard will be shady for a large part of the day, while a south-facing one will enjoy much more sunlight (see opposite).

Your yard's aspect will inform your planting plan, because some plants prefer sun and others thrive in shade. See p.134 for my recommendations for sun- and shade-loving plants. Aspect will also determine where you plan to locate seating, grills, and greenhouses, and where you position ponds and other water features (see p.103).

My second project is on a slope, so the house doesn't cast much shade. Parts of it face south, which maximizes sunlight.

Aspect in the northern hemisphere

Your yard's aspect determines where sun and shade fall within the space as the sun moves across the sky during the day. Understanding your yard's aspect will play a big role in deciding where you site core features, like seating areas, and where to put certain plants.

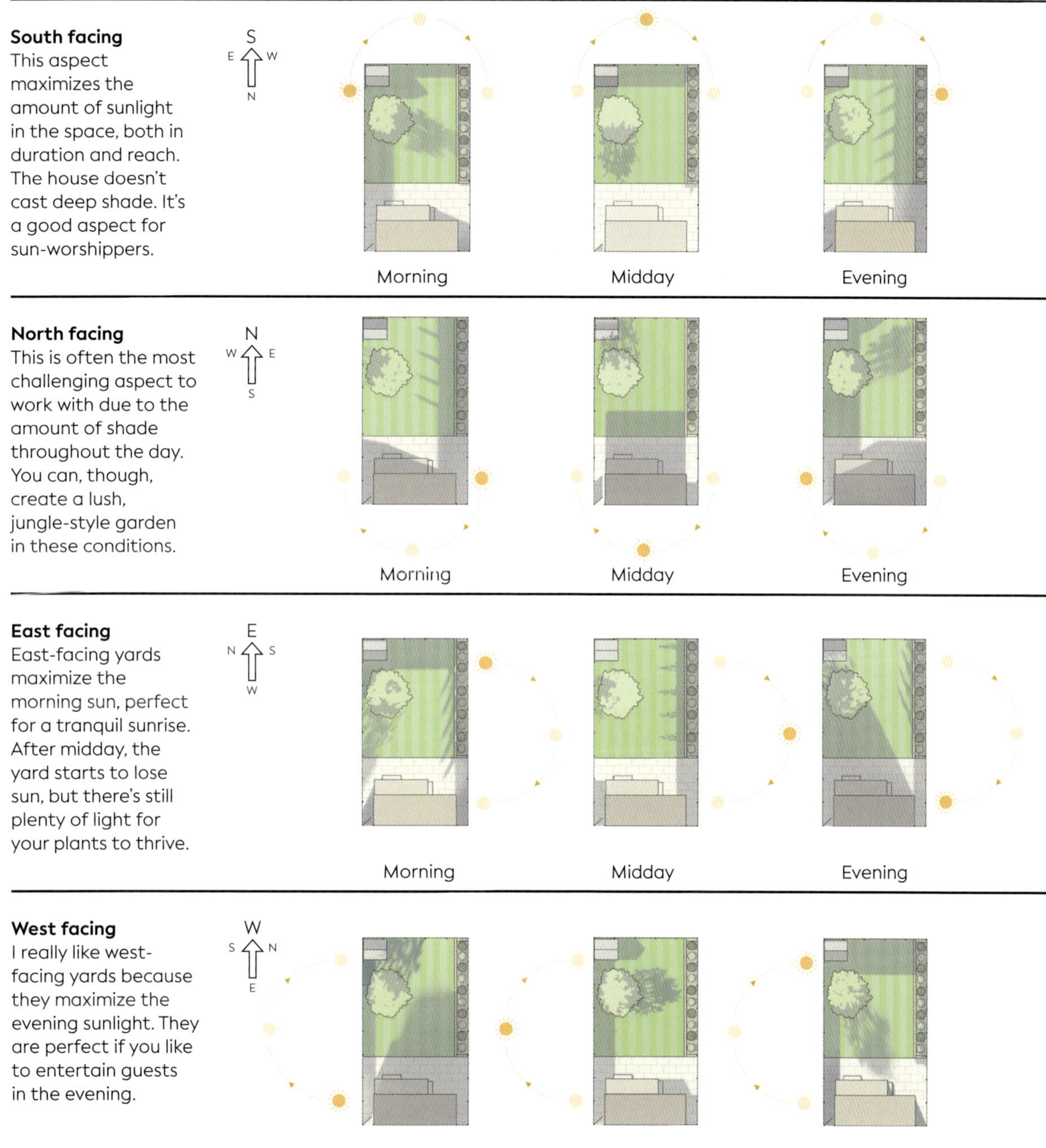

South facing
This aspect maximizes the amount of sunlight in the space, both in duration and reach. The house doesn't cast deep shade. It's a good aspect for sun-worshippers.

North facing
This is often the most challenging aspect to work with due to the amount of shade throughout the day. You can, though, create a lush, jungle-style garden in these conditions.

East facing
East-facing yards maximize the morning sun, perfect for a tranquil sunrise. After midday, the yard starts to lose sun, but there's still plenty of light for your plants to thrive.

West facing
I really like west-facing yards because they maximize the evening sunlight. They are perfect if you like to entertain guests in the evening.

Microclimates

Microclimates are specific, localized areas in an outdoor space that have unique environmental conditions—for example, a shady border next to a north-facing wall or a moist and humid area by a pond or stream.

Every space is unique, and there will always be microclimates based on the orientation of the house, outbuildings, and planting, and the location of boundaries, water, and walls. Woodland or large trees, for instance, create a dry, shady microclimate, which may not be ideal for underplanting.

It's important to understand your yard's microclimates because they will impact what you can plant in certain areas and where you install key features, such as a patio or border. Take the time to walk around your yard, noting sunny and shady spots, damp or boggy areas, and dry shade.

In my second project, I worked with the land, installing a long, curved path over the slope with planting on either side. The result is cohesive, natural looking, and in keeping with the surroundings.

Topography and levels

In almost every yard, there will be varying slopes and differences in levels. Even if the yard appears flat to the naked eye, there will most likely be a change in height. Level changes will impact the overall design and layout of your space, so it's important to understand them before you start the build.

Knowing height differences also allows you to determine how much soil you may need to bring in or take away from the yard, as well as how much leveling you may need to do, either with heavy machinery or, in the case of a small space, by hand.

There are many ways to assess levels and various tools that can help you do it. These range from high-end laser levels to a string and tape measure for basic slope measurements (see opposite).

If your yard is very hilly with complex level changes, it may be worth having a topographical survey carried out by a surveyor. Working smart with your existing levels can save you so much time, effort, and money throughout the project.

You may prefer to work with what you have rather than leveling or tiering slopes. One of the things I learned through my second project was that the more I worked with the natural topography of the land, the easier it was to construct and build my space.

The slope of my yard was quite steep, and many people would choose to tier the space to create flat, even levels. I decided this wasn't an option as it would have involved hours upon hours of work building retaining walls, grading the land with machinery, and bringing in topsoil to create finished levels. The cost would have been exorbitant. Instead, I created a long, curved path. Working with what you have is a good way of saving time, money, and resources.

Measuring a slope
A simple way to measure a slope is to use a string, stakes, and a tape measure to determine the height difference between two or more points on the slope.

TOOLS
String and stakes
Hanging level
Tape measure

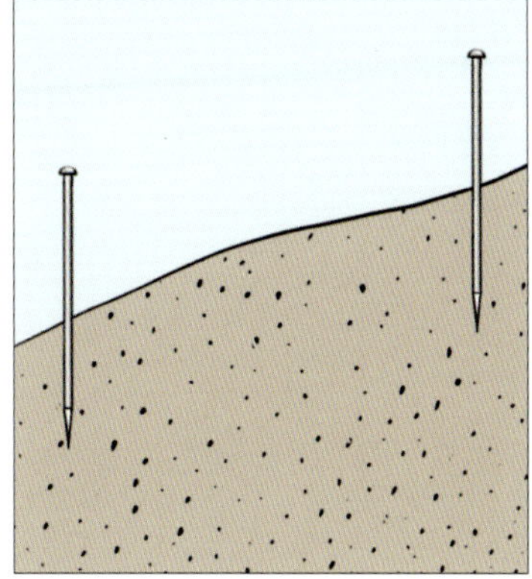

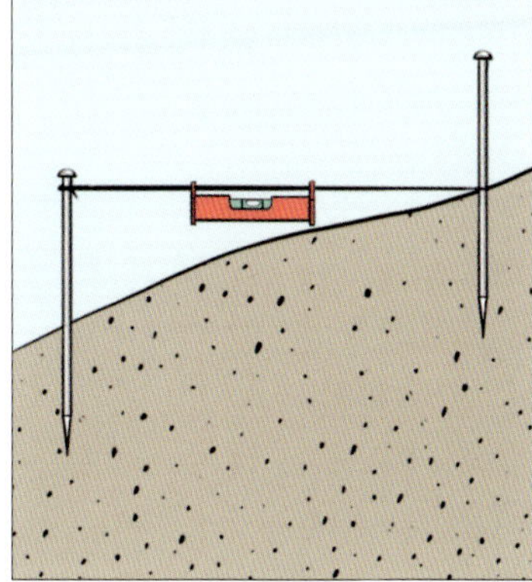

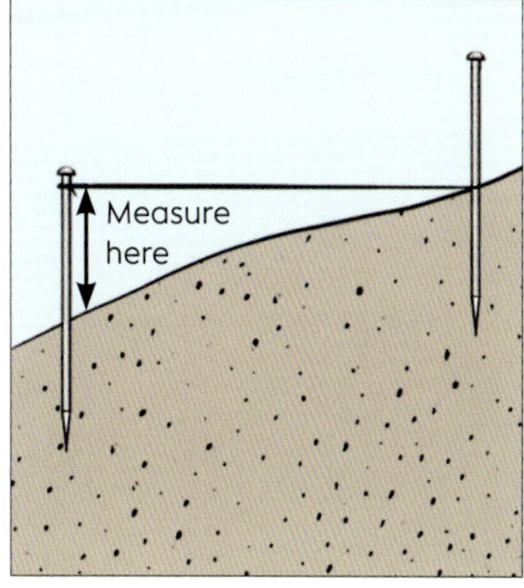

01

Hammer in the stakes

Hammer in stakes at the top and bottom of the slope.

02

Attach a string

Attach a taut string at the base of the top stake and at the top of the bottom stake. Check that it's horizontal with a hanging level.

03

Measure the height

Measure the distance between the string and the ground at the bottom stake to determine the height of the slope.

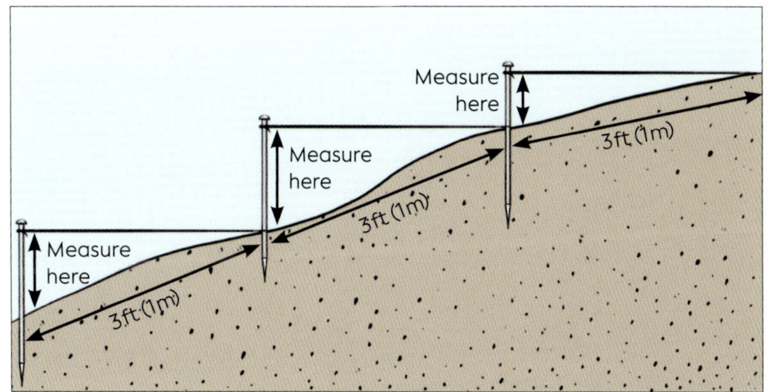

04

Large slopes

If you have a large slope, you can take measurements at intervals, such as every 3 ft (1 m). Add all the measurements together to determine the overall height of the slope.

The practicalities

Once you've assessed your yard's environmental conditions, it's time to address any practical challenges. These include access issues, delivery of materials and removal of waste, and the location of utilities, such as pipes and cables.

Having adequate access for wheelbarrows and machinery will be a huge help when tackling your project.

Access

Good access is crucial for the success and delivery of your project. Can you get machinery and goods easily into the yard, or are you challenged for space? If you have restricted access to the yard, there will always be a creative solution. You may need to find alternative ways in, such as via a neighbor's yard or using a crane to lift materials over your house. Your yard's access will dictate how you plan your project and potentially impact your budget, and you may have to alter your plans based on any access constraints.

Whether you're creating new landscaping from scratch or revamping what's already there, having a clear, accessible site is crucial for your project to run smoothly.

Delivery of materials

From my experience, managing the delivery of goods and materials can get very messy when you're in the middle of a build. Having a spot for deliveries, such as a section of your driveway or a cordoned-off area of your front or backyard, is a must to contain the mess and keep it organized.

Put large sheets of plywood down to protect driveways and other surfaces because aggregate like building sand and cement can get very untidy and stain surfaces. If possible, find a spot where you can have goods delivered that won't prevent you progressing with the various elements of your build.

Removing waste

You will no doubt have to remove excess waste material from the yard to clear the way for new aspects of the build. There are a number of ways you can do this: DIY runs to your local dump or recycling center, dumpster rental, or using a removal service. The DIY run is great if you have minimal waste to get rid of.

Dumpsters are the most commonly used waste-disposal method for domestic home owners, but they can present a challenge if you don't have a driveway to put them on. You may also need a permit for a dumpster, which can be costly. You will need to assess this before you start and factor it into your plans and budget.

Removal services are a cost-effective way to remove large quantities of waste. If you have somewhere to pile all of your waste material neatly and it's accessible from the road, you can use the removal service to collect all the waste.

The location of utilities

Understanding where your main utilities are, such as gas, electricity, and water, or a septic tank or drainage system (see p.14), in and around the house is really important. You don't want to start your project off by digging through a water main or gas pipe. You may prefer to be super cautious and have a utilities survey carried out, or sometimes you can find this information on the deeds or survey data when you originally bought the property.

Plan for lighting

Outdoor lighting is often an afterthought during the planning and build phase, which is a big mistake. Don't leave your decision on whether to include lighting until the end of your project. During the build, you'll have the opportunity to hide and disguise unsightly cables under new patios and paths. Even if you don't think you will need outdoor lighting, it's always a good idea to install electrical conduit so you have the opportunity to add power and lighting at a later point.

Create a site inventory

You will need to decide what will be staying in the yard and what's to be taken away, so create a site inventory list to assist with this.

The legalities

Before embarking on your new landscape project, it's wise to review any potential legal constraints that may influence the decisions you make. There is an entire library of legislation that can impact the house and yard. Here, I've compiled a snapshot of the most common legal situations that can crop up when building and maintaining outdoor spaces.

Property lines

One of the most common legal scenarios is around property lines. You may already know where the property lines are, but it's worth checking the title deeds of your property. Knowing who owns what boundary is critical before you get started because you don't want to tear out someone else's lovely hedge or fence. In addition, you may be expending costs on something that isn't your responsibility to maintain or replace.

Conservation areas

Conservation areas are designed to protect areas of special architectural or historic interest. Reach out to your local planning authority to find out if you are located in a conservation area. If you are, there are limitations on what you can do with the property—for example, you need permission to cut down or trim trees, or even make changes to the external facade of your house. You can find information about controls in your conservation area from your local government, or research what regulations apply in your locality.

Historic zoning

Certain neighborhoods may have special restrictions in place due, for example, to the historic nature of the buildings and homes located there. There may also be a Homeowners Association that imposes restrictions on plantings, outbuildings, fencing, and other aspects of the exterior of the property, such as paint colors.

Restrictions on what you can do with your yard apply if you fall within one of these areas. For example, there are height restrictions for any outbuildings or garden rooms close to property lines, and materials must blend seamlessly with the surrounding environment. Check with your local planning authority or research what might apply in your region.

Watercourses

Natural waters, such as streams and rivers, are considered property of the state in most areas of the United States. There are restrictions on activities within a certain distance of such features. Generally, permission is required for removal of riparian vegetation, for example.

Community standards

Individual communities may have different requirements as to plantings or other landscaping features, especially when these are visible from public streets. As a general rule, however, one can have a yard resembling those elsewhere in the neighborhood without running into permitting and building code issues. Specific types of projects, such as plumbing, electrical, or construction of new buildings will always require permits, regardless of the location.

Other land issues

Depending upon the location, you may not be able to use certain plants in your garden design. For example, many plants considered suitable for landscape use in the UK are prohibited in some areas of the United States because they are considered invasive pest plants. Purple loosestrife, Chinese wisteria, and others pose hazards to native plants. Check your state's Invasive Pest Plant Schedule online.

Your neighbors

Last, but most certainly not least, are your neighbors. One of the most common challenges people face when doing any home or landscaping improvements is complaints from neighbors about noise, dust, loss of views or light, and overlooking. Having your neighbors on board from the beginning will make for a smoother and more pleasant experience. Out of courtesy, you should notify your neighbors of the works taking place, or due to take place, so they are aware of any potential disruptions.

There are some general considerations to be aware of around planting, right to light, and other legislation. For example, if you plant a feature tree next to your property line and it grows taller than 6½ ft (2 m) and starts to block light from your neighbor's main windows, they have every right to lodge a complaint. This also applies if you build a garden room close to the property line and it blocks light to a neighbor's yard. So make sure you do due diligence here and always be considerate of your neighbors before, during, and after the project.

Instinctive design

When I designed and built my first two landscaping projects, I wasn't a qualified garden and landscape designer, but I realized the importance of having a scaled plan of the proposed new project. A scaled plan of the site will help ensure you get the proportions right for each area, such as figuring out how big your patio should be relative to the house, or the size of your planting areas compared to your hard landscaping. However, I don't believe it always needs to be perfectly to scale, because I prefer to work with what I call instinctive design.

My first scaled landscape plan was a very rough sketch, nothing like the ones I do for my clients today. It was a quick drawing roughly to scale, highlighting all of the key areas I wanted to include. It was most certainly not pretty but it did, in essence, depict how I intended the space to flow and the areas I wanted to create. That drawing was based on instinct: how I felt the landscaping should flow based on the existing site conditions, the surrounding environment, and in relation to the house.

If you prefer something more "perfect," there are many design resources available online and in books that will take you through the creation of a full scaled plan from start to finish.

Semi-scaled plan

Using a long tape measure, simply start by taking measurements of the length and width of your space. Then measure the distance from one edge to a key feature, or a few features, that will remain in the new design. This could be an existing path, set of steps, or a shed. Choose a feature relatively close to one edge of your property so you have an idea of where it's positioned relative to the space. Also measure the width and length of the feature. This key feature will provide you with a rough judgment of scale and proportion within the space.

Translate these measurements onto a piece of paper using a scaled rule. Depending on the dimensions of your yard and the size of the paper you're using, you could, for example, use a scale where 1 in represents 1 ft; where ½ in is 1 ft; or where ¼ in is 1 ft. This semi-scaled plan will give you a base outline of your outside space.

Finally, get creative. You have the edges of your property and a key feature in the design measured up and translated to scale on paper. Now you can use some of those to-scale reference points to freehand sketch new features within the space. Use a pencil for your sketching so you can easily make adjustments and overlay new ideas.

Having a partly scaled plan can help you determine how everything else can come together in the new space. It does not need to be perfect! This is a great way to create a rough plan to guide your build, but be prepared to make decisions as you go about measurements for key features, because your plan won't be 100 percent accurate.

The PE teacher approach

If you don't feel confident with creating a scaled plan, or you're just focusing on one area, you can start to measure and mark the areas you want to create using a tape measure, a long hose for curves, and cones for specific zones. This allows you to mark spaces for patios and paths to gauge the scale and how different elements will work within the space.

Once you've marked the areas out, you can use spray paint to mark the ground before you start any ground preparations. This method is very effective and time efficient, especially if the new space has a simple design.

Semi-scaled plan
I made a semi-scaled plan to show how I intended the space to flow and the key features to include. The boundaries are to scale, and I added approximate measurements for new features. Existing features are in color.

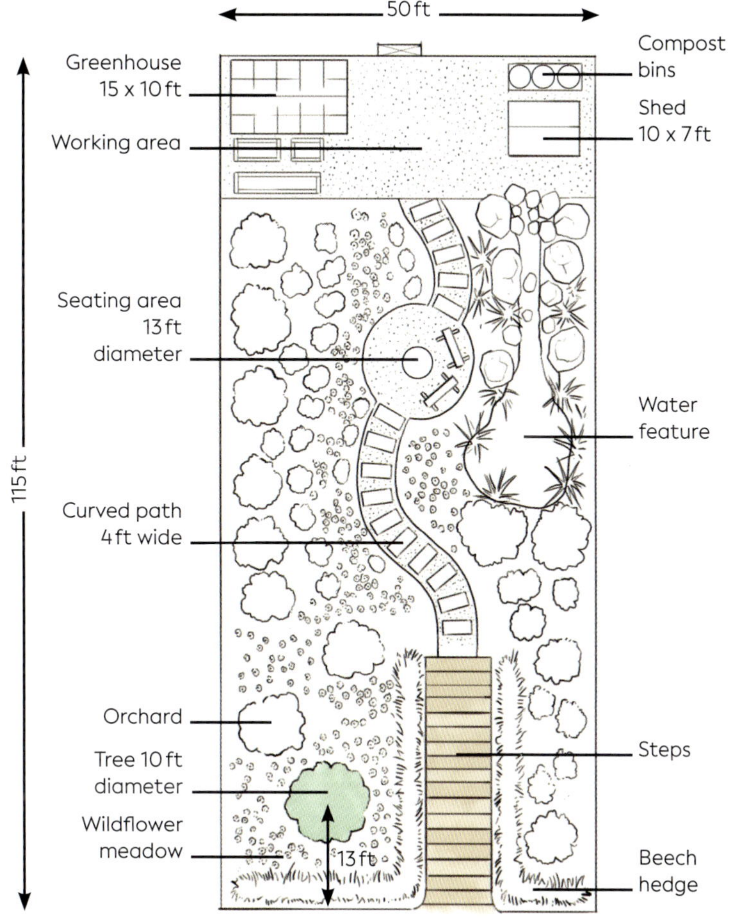

Scale ¼ in
(not shown at actual size)

Your budget

Budgeting for a project seems obvious, but it's often overlooked. Your budget will determine what you can do, and there are always ways to trim down costs as well as alternative, cheaper solutions to achieve the desired aesthetics. Being clear about your budget early on will help you make the right choices further down the line.

Keep on track

My advice is to keep a spreadsheet of running costs, which will help with cash flow. Once the project starts, I recommend you update your budget tracker weekly so you don't forget to add entries for various costs. Keeping on top of your budget will save you money in the long run and keep you on track with your finances. If you have a loose budget and fail to keep track of spending, you may have spent drastically more than you would have liked by the end of the project.

Keeping a spreadsheet of running costs is also a good idea to keep a log of spending for future projects. That way, you can keep builder's merchants consistent with their pricing for repeat orders.

Steps for creating a budget

Full disclosure: finance isn't my strong point, but this isn't particularly complex accounting, and you don't need to be a spreadsheet wizard to create a good working budget. Here are some basic steps to cover.

01

Determine how much money you can put aside and what you are willing to spend on the garden.

02

Research and list in alignment with your plan all the essential expenses for the project. These could include:

- building materials (sand, cement, aggregates)
- tool rental
- waste removal
- hard landscaping finishes
- soft landscaping finishes
- planting
- outdoor structures
- outdoor lighting.

There's little variability in pricing between builder's merchants on standard materials, but it's important to research and gather costs for all of the materials you would like based on your plan. Don't forget about taxes and delivery costs, as these all mount up and can catch you out at times.

03

Assess the costs of materials against your budget by comparing steps 1 and 2. This will give you one of three outcomes: you're under budget (whoopee!), you're in line with your budget (great, let's proceed), or expected costs are over budget, which unfortunately in most cases is the most likely outcome!

If you're under budget, you could consider adding in some wish-list items, such as a water feature or pergola. If you're over budget, you then have two options: you alter your budget and move the goalposts if you have capacity to do so, or you work back through the costs and see where you can make reductions or sacrifices. This could be, for example, changing materials for cheaper options, shrinking the size of the patio, or doing more of the build yourself rather than outsourcing services.

04

Use a spreadsheet to track spending against your budget. Ensure your actual costs are in line with your research and what you've allocated to spend. Simply list the categories and make entries to record purchases and monitor spending. For visual guidance, I like to color code what I've already paid for, outstanding payments, and future costs so I can quickly reference how I'm tracking.

Get three quotes

I recommend getting at least three quotes for professional work, materials, and plants to compare your options across suppliers. It pays to do your due diligence!

Recyclables

It's a good, sustainable, and money-saving practice to make use of existing materials in the garden. If you're taking out an old patio or removing an existing wall, for example, this hardcore can come in handy when you put in foundations for a new patio, shed base, or retaining wall. Once smashed up, it can act as a good subbase (see p.54) for your projects. You wouldn't build directly on it, but it will save you a lot of money when bringing in concrete or subbase aggregate for foundations.

When we had our kitchen renovated, I lifted and repurposed all the kitchen tiles and used them as the subbase for my brick path. It meant I halved the amount of subbase aggregate I needed, which saved me a good $600 on the project.

Upcycling also applies to topsoil, trees, and plants. Good topsoil can be costly, so set it aside where it won't interfere with the build. The cost of mature shrubs and trees is astronomical, so even if they aren't part of your original planting plan, they're valuable assets. Consider reworking the planting design to keep them. And if they absolutely must go, consider gifting them to a friend rather than discarding healthy plants.

Think twice before removing anything—always ask whether it could be reused or repurposed. Create organized, segmented piles of materials and pot up any plants you want to reuse in the new design.

Managing your time

Time management is absolutely critical to ensure your project goes smoothly and that you keep on top of maintenance. If you have a busy lifestyle, you need to be honest about how much time you can spend on the landscaping—time requirements will vary depending on the size of your project and the dimensions and maturity of your space.

There may be parts of a project, for example, that will simply take too long if you tackle them by yourself. Sometimes it's much more time efficient to bring in a professional to help with certain more specialized areas of the build, or laborers who can help with a lot of the graft, such as lugging materials from A to B. This will speed things up and save your project from dragging on. Your time is precious, so use it wisely.

Let's have a look at some ways to manage your time and how you can adapt them depending on what type of gardener you are.

The weekend gardener

Most people who work have a typical week of working Monday to Friday. The weekend is usually when most people manage to carve out time for yard work, but you don't need to dedicate your entire weekend to it. It can be physical—especially if you're building new areas—so it's important you have time to relax and do other things as well. A few hours on a Saturday and Sunday is a good amount of time each week, both to complete projects and to keep on top of core gardening and maintenance jobs, ensuring a happy and healthy yard all year round.

For my landscape projects, I spent most of my weekends completing the work. If I needed a succession of three or four days solid to keep momentum on big projects like building a patio, I planned these projects around national holidays.

Don't forget the need for balance. If you have a family and you don't want to sacrifice your weekends every week, then I recommend either starting at midday on the weekends or committing to every other weekend. That way, you are still present during those precious times with the family. I was pretty fortunate that my little ones loved to get involved. They were mesmerized by the chaos I had created, so it was a lovely way to build memories with them. Getting them involved and making them feel a part of a project just adds that extra-special feeling to the space once it's completed.

Opposite Here I'm constructing a plant support, which I completed in a couple of hours over a weekend.

The weekly gardener

If you have flexible work arrangements or are retired, then creating a weekly gardening schedule will allow you to allocate specific days and times to the garden. That way, you can ensure you stay on top of maintenance all year round and have sufficient time for a building project. A schedule is a great way to plan garden time as long as it's consistent and sustainable in the long term.

Choose days and times that you know you can do and be consistent with your time to achieve the best results. Having a schedule mitigates the job list building up, causing unnecessary anxiety and overwhelm.

Bookending your day

Bookending your day is a great self-improvement strategy that I have used to manage my mental health during stressful periods of my life. So what does it actually mean? Essentially, it's starting and ending the day with an activity or task that you can complete.

This approach can have a positive impact on your mental well-being. Completing a task at the beginning or end of the day provides a sense of accomplishment, which is a great dopamine hit to experience first or last thing. You start and finish the day in a positive headspace.

I currently schedule a 20–30-minute gardening slot before I start work, and again once I've finished work for the day. Breaking it down into two stints like this makes it feel less labor intensive, and it helps me keep on top of the routine gardening tasks like watering, weeding, and pruning, which is especially useful during the summer period.

During the fall and winter months, when it's darker in the mornings and afternoons, I switch up my activities. I start the day with some exercise and finish the day with some greenhouse pottering. If you don't have a greenhouse and would still like to utilize this gardening strategy over fall and winter, you could use your time for planning, sketching out new spaces, thinking about the seeds or bulbs you want to grow, and looking for inspiration to give you a head start in spring.

The 20-minute session

Gardening in a routine of 20-minute high-intensity sessions is good for people who have hectic schedules throughout the week and possibly the weekends too. It's also great for people who would like to use gardening as their exercise routine. Just 20 minutes of intense gardening a day, or every other day, where you really hammer through the job list, is an extremely efficient way to keep on top of things.

Put your gardening gear on, set a timer for 20 minutes, put some headphones in, and simply go for it. It's good to have a plan or list of jobs you want to do in order to maximize your time. For me, it's keeping on top of ruthless weeds like bindweed! Focus on one area or one activity and really give it some elbow grease rather than flitting between jobs.

The power hour

The power hour is another effective way to keep on top of your gardening. It's less intense than the 20-minute session but still requires a good amount of energy and planning. Have your gardening list on hand and see how many jobs you can check off the list within that hour. Plan to have a few power hours scattered throughout the week so you can really make an impact.

Prioritization

Once you've established what's going where, it's time to pull together a project plan, figuring out which areas you will prioritize first so you have a systematic approach for the build. Rank all the different jobs by order of necessity. You may want to get your patio done first, for example, so you can start using it right away, or you may want to work from the back forward so you're not going over newly created spaces.

Creating a project plan

For my projects, I worked from the back of the property toward the house. It meant I had a clean site and I wasn't walking over parts I had recently created. That said, it's not always practical to work like this.

I suggest you always start with the boundaries and then prioritize based on your own situation and what's feasible from there. Breaking down your space into bite-size mini-projects is a great way to stay focused and compartmentalize the build, making it feel less daunting and more achievable. It will also help you visualize the projects and allocate specific months of the year to each section.

Factor in the seasons

Prioritize jobs based on the seasons. If you are giving yourself a calendar year to complete the projects, then allocate certain projects to different times of the year. For example, you do not want to be doing all of your hard landscaping in winter, given the freezing temperatures. It's not the best conditions for making cement and laying patios. It's also considerably less enjoyable doing the more physical parts of the build during those colder months because your hands and feet will get very cold! Choose slightly warmer months for this type of work, such as late fall or very early spring.

Seasonality also impacts planting. Time your planting for optimal times of year, such as spring, summer, or fall. Keep in mind that you will need to pay extra attention to watering in the summer.

Create a list of priorities (see right) to set you up for success further down the line.

TIME MANAGEMENT

- **Decide how much time you have and schedule accordingly.**
- **Allocate time for certain aspects of the project based on optimal seasonality.**
- **Bring in the help of professionals or laborers for time-sapping projects.**
- **Make a list of priorities and create a project plan.**
- **Make time for family by not overcommitting yourself and choosing optimal days and times to focus on the project—it's all about balance.**

PROJECT PLAN

List the jobs in order of importance and allocate them to specific months to give you a clear plan of attack.

PRIORITIES	WHO	TIMELINE
Patio	Self	February–March
Power for lighting	Electrician	February–March
Office	Supplier	March–April
Paths	Self	April–May
Water feature	Self	May
Planting	Self	May–June
Lawn	Self	May–June

Plan to install water features during spring or summer, when weather is optimal. You can plant the space up at the same time to create instant impact.

Your well-being

I passionately believe in the restorative benefits that gardening brings to our mental well-being. Being outside each week and completing little tasks is a fantastic way to nurture the mind. It keeps us moving forward and helps us to remain in the present. Nurturing the garden provides a constant cycle of green therapy, and, even better, you are doing your bit to contribute to a more sustainable lifestyle by growing plants and promoting biodiversity.

Despite the immense benefits of gardening, taking on a project and maintaining the space can be daunting, and some stages may feel overwhelming. Projects do not always go according to plan and you will face challenges along the way, so it's important to protect yourself and recognize that there will inevitably be tricky times to navigate. Be kind to yourself and prioritize your mental and physical well-being.

Tackling your landscaping in small, bite-size projects will help you keep momentum and give you a sense of accomplishment in more frequent doses during the build, which does wonders for your mental health. You should also take a "me day" or have a weekend off here and there to relax, reflect, and unwind. After all, building and maintaining an outdoor space often involve a level of physicality, so it's important to rest your body and recover.

Reflecting on my own experiences, I definitely should have asked for help more often. You don't need to tackle your project completely alone, although, of course, it's fine to do it alone if you prefer. There will be times, though, when having the help of family members or friends can just give you that extra lift or save you many hours lugging materials. Often, people like to be part of a project, so don't be afraid to ask for help along the way.

And finally, remember, Rome wasn't built in a day. Don't rush the journey, enjoy and embrace every stage, especially as you learn and perfect new skills. It's a hugely rewarding process, and when the work is done (although a garden is never truly complete), you will look back and reflect on what was a hugely impactful and positive life experience.

Remember to take time to enjoy the garden and not always be working in it! Create spaces where you can take a moment to sit back, relax, and admire your hard work.

Build

Now that you understand your space and have a strong working plan, you're ready to get going, with each step taking you closer to your dream garden.

In this chapter, we'll look at tackling some of the core hard landscaping projects, from building a patio and a retaining wall to constructing a brick path and steps. There are also step-by-step projects on installing fencing and building structures such as a pergola, raised bed, and compost bay. The projects in this chapter will really start to transform your space.

Ready to go

Outdoor spaces are never ever truly complete—they evolve over time and you will want to make changes. But seeing the structural bones of your garden come together will provide so much satisfaction along the way, and it's a great foundation for the future.

My trusty, rusty wheelbarrow has been with me since the very beginning of building my garden.

Learning on the job

You can go to the nth degree trying to master the art of hard landscaping, but you don't need to spend time finessing how to lay particular paving patterns or learning complex construction methods to achieve a space you can be proud of. The building part of the journey is a learning process—you will acquire skills along the way and acquire a new craft in landscape gardening.

It will be hard work but it's incredibly rewarding, so try not to put too much pressure on yourself to achieve professional results from the get go. It's not about creating an award-winning garden—this is about making a garden that's personal to you and ultimately saves you thousands of dollars on professional landscaping.

That being said, there are options to enhance your skills beyond this book if you would like to take your self-development further. If you want to improve your skills in certain aspects of landscaping, for instance, you could volunteer your services as free labor to a local landscaping company, with a view to learn from them firsthand how to do some of the more intricate aspects of landscaping. There are also many short courses available in bricklaying, carpentry, and stonework.

Take your time

Once you've built some of the core features you want, you will have the blueprint complete with all of the hard work behind you. My recommendation is to take your time with this part of the process, because hard landscaping is a big investment in materials, and you want to make sure you're happy with the end result.

My advice to you is, if you're not happy with something, redo it—later on, your trained eye will always see that slightly uneven slab or wonky brick when your space is complete. Do it nice or do it twice is my motto!

Review your checklist

Before you start building, ensure you have clarity on the following areas:

1. Do you have a vision and goal?
2. Do you understand your environmental conditions?
3. Are you aware of all of the practical challenges you may face, such as delivery of materials?
4. Have you considered any legal issues that may impact your project?
5. Have you got a plan of the space to work with?
6. Have you created a budget tracker?
7. Have you decided how you will manage your time to complete the project?
8. Have you prioritized projects based on access, seasonality, and areas of importance?
9. Finally, have you got a clear wellness strategy in place to ensure you don't suffer from burnout or mental and physical fatigue?

Once you've checked off all of these areas and have a clear plan of action in place, you're ready to begin the adventure!

Essential tools

You will need the right tools for your landscaping journey, whether for the building, planting, or general maintenance. There is a specific set of tools designed for every element of gardening that will be invaluable to you as you progress through each stage of the process. In this section, we will cover what tools you will need for construction, planting, and maintenance, and I highlight some of my go-to tools.

Some investment up front on the right tools will help you out tremendously. You may have a family member or friend who's willing to lend you their tools, but I recommend investing in your own set-up—it's better to have your own personal tools!

Along the way, I've picked up and bought many gardening tools. It's a minor obsession that has seemed to constantly evolve and progress throughout my landscaping and gardening journey. However, there is a set of core tools that I use more frequently than others, and I definitely have some personal favorites.

I find that clipping shrubs to shape with pruning shears is one of the most therapeutic gardening tasks.

Tools for construction

These tools are essential for constructing many of the projects in this book. Remember that you can rent most tools (see below right).

- Buckets
- Builder's trowel
- Cement mixer
- Combi drill
- Concrete breaker
- Crowbar
- Hammer
- Impact driver
- Jointing iron
- Long-handled iron bar
- Lump hammer
- Mattock
- Plate compactor
- Post hole digger
- Sledgehammer
- Spray paint
- String line and pins
- Wheelbarrow

Tools for maintenance

Having the right tools available for maintenance can lighten the load of weekly, monthly, and yearly tasks.

- Composting fork
- Dutch hoe
- Garden snips
- Hand hoe
- Hedge trimmers
- Knee pads
- Lawnmower
- Leaf blower
- Leaf rake
- Loppers
- Power washer
- Pruning saw
- Pruning shears
- Topiary clippers
- Wheelbarrow

Tools for planting

When planting your garden, these tools will be your new best friends, whether for sowing seeds, planting up a border, or laying sod.

- Border spade
- Bulb planter*
- Dibble
- Fork
- Hand fork
- Hori hori
- Post hole digger
- Rake
- Spade
- Trowel

* A bulb planter for planting bulbs in the lawn is preferable to a trowel, because it is designed to make light work of planting through turf. Turf is tough and requires some elbow grease to remove for planting.

TOOL RENTAL

At times, the cost of buying versus renting doesn't make financial sense, especially if you only need the tool for one weekend. You may need to rent specific tools, such as heavy-duty machinery and power tools, for certain points of the project. Many builders' merchants offer tool-rental services or there are specialized rental companies. It's worthwhile noting down who they are in your area because you will likely need to rent certain tools throughout your build.

My top-five tools

Given the time, money, and effort they have saved me over the years, I want to highlight these specific tools. Sometimes you will need heavy machinery like diggers, but I built my first two gardens with no heavy machinery, just a core set of tools and plenty of elbow grease!

Post hole digger

A post hole digger is a versatile, long-handled tool with two articulated, shovel-like blades, which makes it easy to dig deep holes in tough terrain. If you're building a fence or installing a pergola or arch, this nifty tool will help you dig deep holes with half the effort of using a spade or pickax. I garden on solid chalk, and even in these conditions, the post hole digger helps me reach the depths needed for concreting posts into the ground.

I also use a post hole digger for planting. If I'm planting a large shrub or tree and need to excavate a sizable hole, I turn to this tool rather than a spade. It gets the job done a lot quicker than using a traditional spade. It's also a fantastic workout for your shoulders, triceps, and back.

Long-handled iron bar

This tool is essentially a long piece of iron with a chisel-like end, designed to tackle tough ground. It isn't your standard off-the-shelf tool, but it is an absolute game-changer for landscaping.

I've used it many times when I've needed to lever a large piece of concrete out of the ground or smash through some tree roots. It's the ideal tool for stubborn concrete, such as wall and patio foundations. Given the weight of it, this tool will be your best friend for moving those stubborn objects or unwanted plants. You do need strong wrists, though!

Mattock

The mattock is similar to a pickax except that one side has a larger horizontal blade, which is perfect for smashing through stubborn roots and digging trenches. The other side resembles a traditional pickax, designed for tackling tough ground.

The amount of hours I've used this tool is countless—it's my go-to tool in the shed. I dig trenches with it, remove stubborn shrubs, and clear gardens, and it's a great tool for digging and demolishing. I would choose this over a pickax any day of the week, because I can achieve a lot with it in a very short period of time. It's also a great stress reliever when you swing it around, but just be sure to wear safety boots when you do!

Hori hori

The hori hori is a multipurpose digging or weeding knife that originated in Japan. The word "hori" derives from the Japanese for "to dig." This tool is a favorite among gardeners because it's versatile and easy to use.

I use it for weeding, planting bulbs and small perennials, and creating drills for sowing seed directly into the ground. Its sharp edge is also ideal for cutting roots, splitting bulbs, opening bags, and so on. It's my trusty companion, along with my pruners.

Cement mixer

A cement mixer is powered by either gasoline or electricity and you use it for assisting in making concrete or mortar. During the build of my garden, I soon realized that the cost of renting one over several weekends slowly mounted up, so I picked up a new one and I've had it for many years now. It was one of my best investments due to the sheer amount of landscaping I undertook. It's a bit worse for wear but I've used it a lot, and it's saved me so much money, time, and effort compared with renting one.

If you are building a new garden, then I highly recommend you purchase a cement mixer, either new or secondhand. The only drawback is that you will need somewhere to store it, preferably a dry spot, to keep it in good working order.

Concrete and mortar

For many of the build projects in this book, you'll need to work with concrete and mortar. Here, we'll look at the differences between them, what they're used for, and how to make them.

A wheelbarrow full of mortar, which is a perfect consistency for brick- and blockwork.

What is concrete?

Concrete is a solid construction material that is produced by mixing cement, ballast (known as aggregate), and water together. Ballast is comprised of sand and gravel. You can either buy washed gravel and sand separately to mix with cement for making concrete, or you can buy ballast that has a ready-made ratio of sand to gravel, which makes life that much easier when it comes to making your mix.

When you mix those key ingredients together, it sparks a chemical reaction that results in the mixture hardening into a solid, almost rocklike structure. Given the strength and durability of concrete, it's used in a multitude of ways and makes a solid foundation on which to build.

What is mortar?

Mortar is a binding material made by mixing cement and building sand or sharp sand. It's used for building all kinds of structures, such as a wall or patio. It bonds materials such as bricks, concrete blocks, and natural stones together to provide strong structural integrity. It's essentially the glue binding individual elements together to create a larger structure. Mortar is used widely in the construction of homes and gardens all over the world.

WHAT IS CEMENT?

Cement is the binding agent for both concrete and mortar. It's predominantly made from limestone, clay, or shale, and is a fine, gray powder that usually comes in 55-lb (25-kg) bags. Once mixed with water, a chemical reaction occurs, called hydration, which causes the mixture to harden over time.

Alternatives

Concrete and mortar are considered bad for the environment because of the significant carbon dioxide emissions created during production, their use of nonrenewable, natural resources, high water demand, and their detrimental effects on local ecosystems.

There are many alternative ways to build a beautiful space without using concrete or mortar. For example, instead of laying stone slabs on a full mortar bed for paths and patios, you can simply lay them on compacted crushed stone or sharp sand, as long as the edges are well reinforced. You could also opt for more natural, organic paths by using just cardboard with wood chips on top and logs for edging, which is a great way to create quick and easy pathways without any concrete at all.

For retaining earth, natural dry stone walls and gabion baskets filled with stones, or even stacked log walls, are all options that don't require concrete foundations.

With foundations for structures such as greenhouses or sheds, consider using gravel or paving slabs laid on a sand base instead of concrete.

When to build

The freezing temperatures and significant amount of rainfall make winter a really tricky time to take on the larger and more complex hard landscaping projects, especially if cement and mortar are involved. Freezing can disrupt the hardening process, making the mix unusable. Spring and summer are the optimal times, and even in the fall you'll have time to squeeze in a project before that slightly more challenging period.

It's best to do hard landscaping projects on a dry day when you have a good 48 hours of no rain forecast. If it does rain after you've finished and before the concrete or mortar has dried, you can protect brickwork or freshly laid paving with a tarp.

How to make concrete and mortar

If you've never made concrete or mortar before, it can seem like quite a daunting task at the beginning. Once you've got the hang of it and understand the basics around ratios and mix consistency, it becomes second nature, and you will become pretty adept in no time at all. Understanding the fundamentals around making concrete and mortar is essential if you're planning on building garden walls, or installing fencing, patios, and paths.

The mix

First, you need to determine your mix, which will depend largely on what you're using your mortar or concrete for. The process of making concrete and mortar is the same—it's just the contents and consistency that are different. For concrete, you want a much wetter, stronger mix than for mortar. For mortar to be used on standard brickwork, you're aiming for a much stiffer but workable consistency. Don't overfill the drum—working in smaller batches will ensure mix consistency and quality.

Here are some mixes for common outdoor build jobs:

Footings for walls and foundations for sheds and outbuildings
Concrete: 1 part cement and 5 parts ballast

Brick and concrete blockwork
Mortar: 1 part cement and 4 parts building sand

Edging and paving
Mortar: 1 part cement and 4 parts sharp sand

It's really important to stick to the ratios, much like sticking to the exact measure of ingredients required in a recipe. Use a leveled-off bucket to measure each part of the formula, which will ensure your mix is consistent every time.

If you're only making a small amount of concrete or mortar, making a hand mix in a wheelbarrow will save you the time and effort of setting up and cleaning your mixer.

Use a cement mixer for larger projects that require more volume of either mortar or concrete.

The process

01

Make sure your ballast, sand, cement, and water are easily accessible. Set up your cement mixer on a level, even surface.

02

If I'm working on a very small project and only need a tiny amount of mortar or concrete, I just hand mix it in a wheelbarrow or bucket. It saves the whole rigmarole of setting up and cleaning the cement mixer. If you're using a mixer, always start by adding a little water to the drum, which will help stop the dry mix from sticking to the inside.

03

I recommend adding half of the ballast or sand first with the cement, let that mix for a good few minutes, and slowly add some water to loosen up the mixture. Add the rest of the aggregate and let it work itself in.

04

When using a mixer, turn it off and make sure you are happy with the mix and consistency. Place a wheelbarrow directly underneath the drum and tip the mixer to empty it. The contents will travel quite a distance, so be careful as you empty the drum—you don't want to splash everything in sight and create a mess. Use concrete or mortar within the hour, before it starts to set.

05

Always rinse the mixer or wheelbarrow immediately after use. Add a bucket of water and some loose gravel to break off any stubborn bits of cement. Empty the drum or wheelbarrow and wipe clean.

Premade concrete

Some of the projects in this book call for a ready-made mix. For example, quick-setting concrete is used for setting wooden, metal, and concrete posts into the ground, and you simply add water to the mix. It sets in a few minutes and is a quick and easy material to use. As a rule of thumb, you'll need about one 44-lb (20-kg) bag per post.

Concrete pump and pour

If you have a particularly large area for concreting, such as the foundations for a large garden office or long retaining walls, it may be more time efficient to hire the services of a concrete pump and pour. You pay for your concrete from a local concrete supplier, and your chosen mixture arrives on a large truck with a pump to pour your concrete wherever you need it. The pump has a large, hose-like attachment that runs along the ground and around obstacles, which is particularly handy for areas with challenging access. This service is a great way to save time on labor and to tackle big areas of your project at one time.

To help you decide which option would be best for your project, calculate how much concrete you need—a standard mixer drum holds 29–35 gallons (130–160 liters). Also consider the time it will take to mix by hand or with a mixer versus bringing in a concrete pump.

Boundaries

Boundaries play a big role in the appearance of your space and are often visible from many parts of the property. The most commonly used boundaries are walls, fencing, and hedging, and they all create a different impact and feel. In this section, we will look at how to build a contemporary wooden fence. On pp138–141, there is a step-by-step project on how to plant a hedge.

Boundaries define the space and are often the first thing people see when they arrive at a property. It's important to give them the focus and care that you do with other aspects and features. Choose a boundary that fits the aesthetic of your space as well as your budget.

Walls

Walls are the most permanent solution. They take longer to install and are much more expensive than traditional fencing and hedging. The range of materials for walling is extensive, from traditional brickwork to natural stone. Elaborate natural stones are more expensive and labor intensive to lay than standard bricks. A cost-effective and time-saving option is to use prefabricated stone cladding panels or similar products.

Opposite, clockwise from top left A traditional wood fence, a large brick wall softened by planting, a contemporary slatted cedar fence, and a wall used as a backdrop to elevate planting in the foreground.

Fencing

Fencing is quick to install, less expensive than walls, and can, over time, blend well with its surroundings. Fencing ranges from natural timbers and composites to metallic fences. Timber fencing is the most commonly used because it's readily available and quick to install. A cedar slatted fence, for example, adds a contemporary feel and a touch of class. The downside is the upkeep and longevity, because timber tends to rot over time. Composite fencing has the look of timber and lasts longer, but is more expensive. Steel fencing, such as woven Corten steel panels, is far more durable than timber, but comes with a higher price tag.

Hedging

Hedging is the natural solution, requiring annual maintenance. It provides a beautiful backdrop for planting and an ecosystem to attract wildlife. Hedging is the cheapest solution, but it needs time to fully form, unless you dig deep and buy mature hedging plants, in which case, the impact is almost instantaneous.

How long it takes 1–2 weekends **Best time to do** spring, summer, or fall

Project
How to install a slatted fence

Installing a fence is incredibly rewarding and satisfying. It's one of those DIY projects that doesn't necessarily require professional help, especially if it's just a small fence. Here, I'll walk you through building a slatted, contemporary-style fence using treated timber posts and cedar battens.

Before you start

Make sure the space where your fence will be installed is clear of vegetation and any obstructions. Measure the length of your fence line to determine how many posts you'll need. For standard fences, upright posts should be spaced about 6 to 7¾ft (1.8 to 2.4 m) apart. Also decide on the height of your fence to determine how many battens you'll need for the slats. Precut your wood to size.

A nail gun is a useful tool for this project as it's quicker than using a drill. They are very expensive to buy so you could consider renting one.

Refer to p.163 for tips on repairing an existing fence.

MATERIALS

Wall plate: 7¾ft x 4 in x 2 in (2.4 m x 100 mm x 50 mm) (optional)

Wall plugs 4 x 2¼ in (100 x 55 mm) (optional)

Masonry screws: 3½ x ¼ in (90 x 6 mm) (optional)

Treated fence posts: 7¾ft x 4 in x 4 in (2.4 m x 100 mm x 100 mm)

1 bag concrete mix per post

Timber screws: 1½ x ⅛ in (38 x 4 mm)

Cedar battens: 6 ft x 1¾ in x ¾ in (1.8 m x 45 mm x 20 mm)

TOOLS

Tape measure

Circular saw or handsaw

String line and pins

Hammer

Spray paint

Electric screwdriver

Post hole digger

Spirit level

Pencil

Drill and drill bit or nail gun

½-in (1-cm) spacers

Slatted fence
Timber posts are concreted in place and cedar battens are attached horizontally to create the individual bays. It's important that at least 24 in (600 mm) of the posts are concreted into the ground for stability.

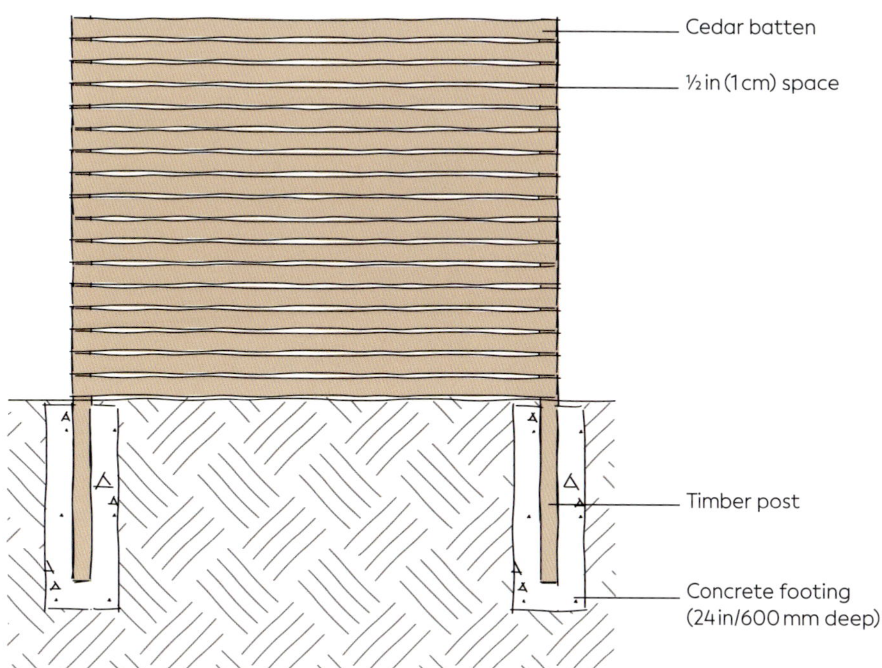

01

Mark the post positions

Run a string line along the area where your new fence will go. Measure along the length of the line, marking the spot where each post will go with spray paint.

02

Attach the wall plates

If you are affixing the fence to a wall at one or both of the ends, attach a wall plate with masonry screws and wall plugs to the wall. If not, proceed to step 3.

03

Dig holes for the posts

Using a post hole digger, dig holes that are at least 24 in (600 mm) deep for the posts.

04

Install the posts

Place your first post in its hole. If it's too tall, you can saw it down at the end of the project. Use a level to check that it's vertically straight. Put water into the hole first, then pour concrete mix in and water as you go, following the packet instructions.

05

Check the levels

Before the concrete mix sets, check again that the post is level. Wash the post down so it's not stained by concrete mix. Repeat the process for the rest of the posts.

06

Install the battens

Start from the bottom so you can stack the cedar battens. They will sit flush with the face of each vertical post. Position the end of a batten in the middle of the bay post, where it will meet the batten of the adjoining bay. Battens at the end sit flush with the end of the wall plate or end post. Mark the batten with a pencil where it will attach to the posts.

Drill pilot holes into both ends of the batten, using the pencil marks as a guide. Drill one end into place with a timber screw or use a nail gun. Then check it's horizontal with a level before screwing in the other end.

If the ground is uneven, use a handsaw or circular saw to trim the bottom slat with an angled cut to fit.

07

Fill the first bay

Continue adding the battens. Use ½-in (1-cm) spacers to get a consistent gap between battens, which will allow space for natural movement of the timber. Ensure each batten is level and aligned.

08

Fix supporting plates

Once you've finished filling a bay, fix a batten as a supporting plate at the back and in the middle of each bay with timber screws. This will help keep the battens aligned and the fence sturdy during windier months of the year. Continue this process until you've filled all the bays.

09

Attach capping timber

Attach battens as capping timber where the horizontal battens meet on the bay posts. Affix two battens as corner caps at the wall plate and/ or end posts for a neater look.

Tip

If you don't want to see through the fence, staple black membrane to the posts at the back of the fence. You can attach battens on the other side too if you wish.

And that's it! Once you're done, step back and admire your brand-new fence. Putting plants next to it will soften the overall look and feel.

Patios and paths

Patios and paths are essential in almost every space. They are often the most-used features, so material selection and layout are absolutely key. They will most likely be your largest investment in materials and time spent on construction—the bigger the patio or path, the higher the cost and the more time you will need to dedicate to the project. In this section, we'll look at step-by-step projects of building a natural stone patio and installing a brick paver path.

This small patio features Dutch pavers laid in a herringbone pattern for a timeless look.

Patios

Patios can extend your interior into the outdoors. Using materials that match those of the house in your external paving is a great way to blend the space, making it feel unified and creating a blurred line between the house and yard. This is particularly effective with bifold doors, where the patio and house floor are the same height.

Your patio space should be proportionate to the size of the house. A small patio next to a large house will look out of place, so try to size your patio according to the dimensions of your house. The size of your patio should also be determined by how you intend to use it. Will you have a dining area? Will there be an outdoor kitchen? Will you use it for table tennis? If you know you are going to use it for a broad range of activities, it's better to go slightly bigger, so you don't regret not having enough space further down the line.

Paths

Paths define the journey of your landscaping. They take you to and from destinations, connecting spaces within the design. I break paths down into primary paths and secondary paths. Primary paths are your core paths, such as one central path from your patio to the back of the yard where there's a destination, such as a log cabin. Secondary paths branch off this, and they may be stepping stones in a border or mulch paths leading to woodland areas of a garden. I always start by defining where my primary paths are going and then I work out my secondary paths from there.

Types of path

Brick paths are a traditional way to add a timeless look and feel to your outside space. The variation of bricks available is vast, and there are brick colors/finishes applicable to any setting. Brick paths are a good durable option because they have a solid construction and can take heavy footfall and wheelbarrow use. They're a great option for primary paths, meandering through a space or leading to and from key focal points. They add warmth, texture, and a rustic charm.

Wood chip paths are the most sustainable option because there's no concrete or cement involved. They blend seamlessly with nature and are good for secondary paths, such as running through a woodland area where hard-landscaped paths might look out of place. You can buy wood chips from a local garden center or bulk loads from larger builders' merchants. I recommend you get friendly with your local tree surgeon, because they often pay to get rid of chipped wood, so most would be happy to deliver a truck load on your driveway for free! If you're looking for a natural look with ease and simplicity of installation, wood chip paths are a great option.

Gravel paths are popular thanks to the ease of construction, variety of decorative stone available, cost, and, above all, their permeability. Gravel allows rainwater to flow into the soil below, replenishing groundwater and reducing the risk of flooding. Gravel paths can be used as primary or secondary routes, are quick to install once you've got your edges in, and look fantastic combined with other materials.

Gravel and wood chips are less accessible than brick paths for wheelchair users and wheelbarrows, and they may migrate into other areas, which can look untidy.

Time and cost

Consider time and cost: laying a gravel path, for instance, will take considerably less time and cost significantly less than laying a brick path. You may only have a weekend to complete certain areas, so you should make material decisions based on the time you can allocate. Also take into account the physicality involved, based on your levels of fitness, and your budget.

Foundations

You need solid foundations for paths and paving for longevity. It's worth investing time and effort on getting the foundations right before you lay your surface layer.

Typical path and patio foundations consist of a membrane to stop the subsoil mixing with the subbase; a solid subbase material, such as concrete or crushed limestone, also known as crusher run; and a mortar or sand layer. Judge your footings by the ground you are working with. If you have solid ground, for instance, such as flint and chalk, you may be able to skip installing a subbase for a gravel path.

Calculating materials

To determine the quantity of materials you'll need, first calculate the area of the patio or path by multiplying the length and width in feet or meters to give you the square feet or square meters. To calculate the volume of subbase or aggregate needed for foundations, multiply the area by the depth of the subbase to give you the cubic feet or cubic meters required. For crushed limestone, you'll need about 1.8–2.2 tons per 35 cubic feet.

Most builders' merchants have calculators on their website for working out quantities of materials (see p.186). When ordering materials, allow 10 percent extra for wastage.

Choosing materials

Another common denominator for paths and patios is material choices. There is a broad range of aggregates, stones, and paving options on the market, and it can be confusing to decide which would be best for your project. Factors to consider include cost, longevity, maintenance, and matching the material to your house, surrounding landscape, or local natural stone.

Permeability and drainage

During the planning phase, you considered what environmental challenges you may face, including drainage (see p.14).From a sustainability perspective, one of the biggest factors to consider alongside the aesthetic appeal is whether or not you're looking for a permeable or non-permeable surface. A permeable material allows water to pass through it. Most natural stones and aggregates are permeable unless they are sealed. Artificial products like porcelain, for example, offer no permeability.

You can also have a permeable or non-permeable subbase and joints between paving. Sand is typically used between joints and under block-paved driveways or brick paths instead of mortar, creating a permeable subbase and joints. A concrete subbase is non-permeable, and very strong mortar joints are less permeable than sand.

Permeable construction is a more sustainable method because it allows water to flow back into the ground, reduces water runoff, and will ultimately lower your costs on maintenance.

If you opt for a non-permeable surface, you will need to think about drainage. When

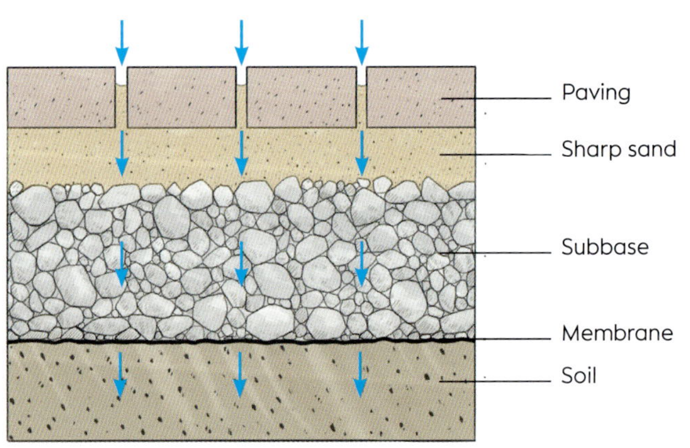

Permeable construction
This brick-paved path is laid on a bed of sharp sand with sand brushed in the joints, allowing rainwater to penetrate and go back into the water table.

it rains, you will need a channel to direct excess surface water into a new or existing drainage system to avoid flooding. It's amazing just how much surface water a patio collects when it's pouring down rain!

You need to think about each aspect before construction. It could go wrong, for instance, if you install a non-permeable subbase with permeable paving and joints. Rainwater will seep down onto the subbase and may freeze in cold months, causing the paving to crack or pop off the mortar bed.

If you have any doubts regarding the permeability of your project, it's worth getting some advice from a professional—it could be a costly mistake otherwise.

Pavers
Very much on trend, brick and Dutch pavers come in all sorts of colors and finishes.

Brick paver

Dutch pavers

Path and paving materials
There is a wide variety of finished materials to choose from, including natural and artificial stone. Here the cheapest materials are on the left with the more expensive ones on the right.

Gravel

Concrete

Sandstone

Limestone

Porcelain

Slate

Yorkstone

Cobbled sett

Natural stone cladding

Cheapest materials → **Mid-range materials** → **More expensive materials**

Combining materials

Combining materials is another key thing to consider. It creates visual interest and helps to soften all the hard landscaping elements, turning what could be considered uninteresting patios and paths into statement features. Opting for one material for your patio, paths, and walls could appear quite stark and lack character.

A good rule of thumb is to work with a combination of three different hard landscaping materials—any more than this can have the opposite effect of feeling messy and overwhelming. Working with different materials can also help you distinguish different zones and areas.

Combining different textures is aesthetically pleasing, brings more depth to the space, and creates a more cohesive overall design. For example, I have combined Dutch pavers with Yorkstone and Cotswolds chips in my courtyard, materials that have different textures but complementary colors.

A combination of Dutch pavers, Yorkstone, and gravel breaks up the area and creates visual interest.

Combining materials can also help you achieve the look you want in a more budget-friendly way. For example, you may wish to have a large walkway or seating area paved with beautiful Dutch pavers, but the cost per square foot across the entire space can be very expensive. Instead, you could break the section down by having Dutch pavers in key areas and an alternative, more cost-effective material like gravel in the other spaces. If the materials complement each other, you can still create a stunning space, but you've saved yourself plenty of time and money along the way.

Paving styles

The way in which paving is laid can make a big impact visually, and it also helps to break up an expansive patio area. There are multiple ways to lay a patio or brick or stone path, from crazy paving to contemporary Ibiza-inspired patios. Ultimately, the way and style in which you lay paving will be reflective of your tastes and preferences.

Bricks and pavers are great for creating intricate details in paths and patios, and you can apply the different patterns used in bricklaying to lay them. Being creative with the laying bonds can help to form seamless transitions between different areas, and you can encourage movement by laying in the direction of travel.

Materials and the way they're laid can influence the style of a space. For example, if you have a lovely reclaimed red brick laid in a herringbone pattern, it will make the space feel quite traditional. Alternatively, large 36 x 24 in- (900 x 600 mm-) slab paving laid in a standard stretcher bond fashion will create quite a contemporary look and feel.

Large paving patterns
These are some of the more commonly used laying patterns for large-format paving.

Stretcher bond

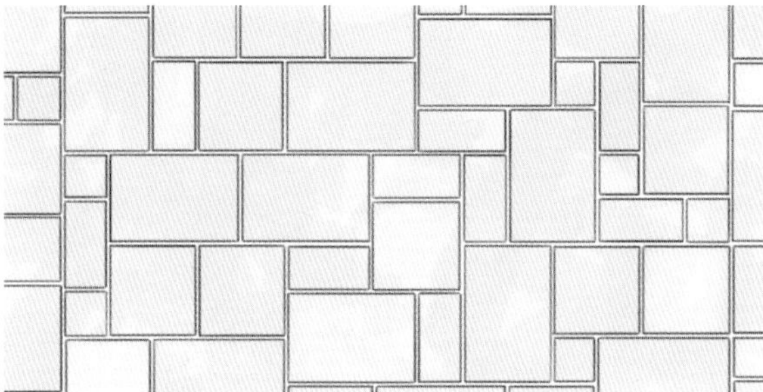
Random-size slabs

One-third offset running bond

Stack bond

Small paving patterns
Given the difference in size, more intricate laying details can be achieved using small-format paving than with large-format paving.

Herringbone

Small stretcher bond

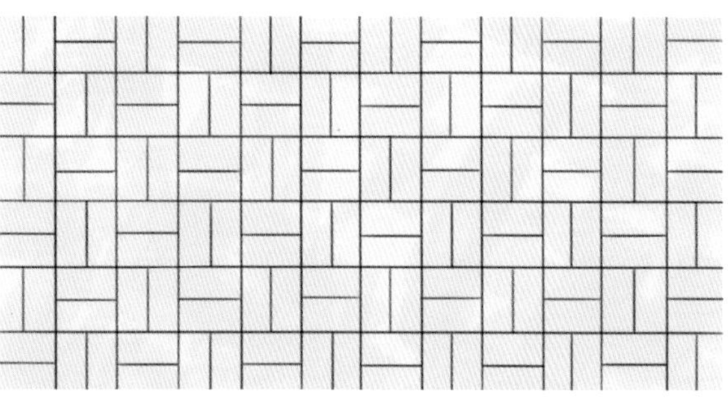
Basket weave

90-degree herringbone

How long it takes 1 weekend+ **Best time to do** spring, summer, or fall

Project
How to lay a patio

Building a patio is often one of the bigger projects you'll take on, given the preparation and time involved. While it might seem daunting, laying a patio isn't overly complicated—you just need a good grasp of some of the basic principles before diving in.

Before you start

You will need to calculate how much subbase material you need, depending on the patio size and subbase thickness (see p.54). Aim for a subbase thickness of 4–6 in (100–150 mm).

Depending on the size of your patio, this stage can be labor intensive, so consider getting help to transport the subbase material to the patio area. Don't be afraid to ask friends and family to help—now would be a good time to save your back!

Decide on the final height of your patio—this determines the level of excavation needed for a solid subbase. Calculate the total thickness of the patio, including subbase, membrane, mortar bed, and slabs, to determine how much ground you will need to excavate. Setting the height correctly can save you from having to bring in extra material to build up the levels.

Make sure you factor in the width of your joints when you calculate materials for the project.

MATERIALS

- Geotextile membrane
- Crushed limestone for the subbase
- Sharp sand
- Cement
- Paving slabs
- Styrene butadiene rubber (SBR) primer
- Stone sealer (optional)
- Building sand

TOOLS

- Tape measure
- String line and iron pins
- Builder's square
- Spade
- Wooden pegs
- Marker pen
- Lump hammer
- Long level
- Wheelbarrow
- Rake
- Power compactor or hand tamper
- Buckets
- Cement mixer or wheelbarrow
- Builder's trowel
- Spacers (optional)
- Rubber mallet
- Angle grinder and PPE (goggles, ear protectors, mask, gloves, and steel toecaps)
- Pointing trowel
- Pointing iron
- Soft brush

Patio cross-section
This patio is laid on a non-permeable foundation with a mortar layer and mortared joints. You can choose to add brick edging, as here, or simply use regular slabs for the edges.

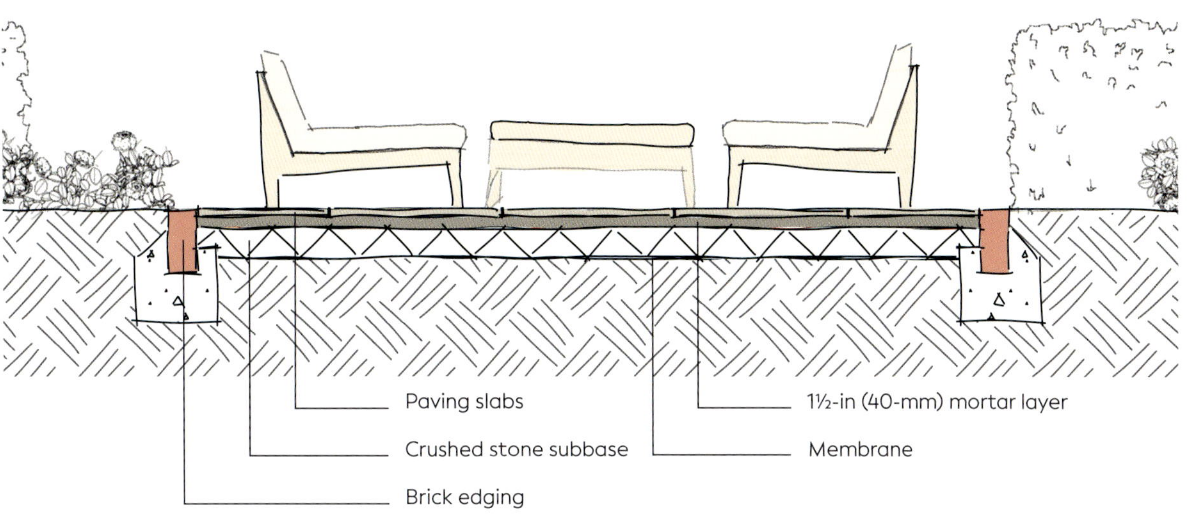

01

Set out the site

Start by marking out the area using iron pins and a string line. Make sure your corners are square (see right).

SQUARING THE CORNERS

To ensure your corners are square, you can use the 3:4:5 method for larger spaces or a builder's square for smaller areas. For the 3:4:5 method, measure in multiples of 3, 4, and 5. For example, measure 12 in (30 cm) across one length of the edge and mark it using a pen. Measure 16 in (40 cm) across the perpendicular edge and mark it with a pen. Measure a line from both markers (to create a triangle)—it should be 20 in (50 cm) if the corner is square.

02

Excavate the area and install membrane

Dig to the depth you have calculated you need for your patio. Next, lay and install a geotextile membrane cut to the appropriate size of your space. If it's windy, you could hold it in place with bricks. It will stop your subbase material from combining and mixing in with the soil beneath, keeping structural integrity to your foundations.

03

Set out the heights and levels

Use wooden pegs to mark and set out the height and levels of your patio. Installing the subbase at the right height with the correct fall (see box opposite) now will make laying the mortar bed and slabs easier later.

Start by driving a peg into the ground closest to wherever your finished height reference point is, which could be the adjoining house, an outbuilding, or a string line, as here. Drive this peg into the ground until you reach the finished height.

Then mark on your peg each of the different layers: bottom of slab, mortar bed, and crushed limestone.

04

Establish the fall rate

Once your first peg is at the correct height, continue to knock in a row of pegs across the width of the patio, ensuring they are placed a minimum of 3 ft (1 m) apart. Use a long level to align each peg horizontally, ensuring they are level.

With the first row of pegs in place and level, you now want to establish the fall rate to make sure your subbase is at the correct gradient (see box opposite). Insert the next row of pegs in front, slightly deeper, depending on the desired fall. For a small patio, you can work to an offset bubble on a level to provide you with an adequate fall for drainage.

05

Install the subbase

With the pegs and levels set, it's time to lay the subbase. Here I'm using 6 in (150 mm) of chipped limestone. Use a wheelbarrow to tip the material into place, spreading it evenly to the height of the subbase marked on your pegs. Once the area is covered, use a rake to level it out.

Tip

If you are installing the patio next to the house, the finished patio height should be at least two brick courses below the house's damp-proof course.

CALCULATE THE FALL

The patio should slope away from any adjoining buildings to avoid water pooling near the foundation. Direct surface water into a drainage channel that connects to your existing drainage system, or onto a lawn or planting bed if it's a smaller patio and drainage is adequate.

For most patios, you'll want a fall ratio of between 1:60 and 1:100, or ½ in (1 cm) of fall for every 24–39 in (60–100 cm) of paving. For small patios, you can use the offset bubble on a level as a guide for the fall. For a smooth stone, the bubble needs to touch the inside of the line on the level. For a riven or more natural stone with undulations, you will need a greater fall and the bubble can go over the line by a quarter.

For a larger patio space, divide the length of your patio in inches (millimeters) by the desired fall rate, such as 1:80, to calculate the exact height difference for the fall. For example, the patio I am working on is 106 in (2,700 mm) long and I am aiming for a fall rate of 1:80. So the calculation is 106 (2,700) divided by 80, which is 1⅓ in (33.75 mm). That is the exact height difference required from one end of the patio to the other to create the 1:80 fall rate.

If you want to take the precise route, rather than using the offset bubble in the level, mark the height differences in exactly the same way using wooden pegs and run a string line from point A to B. This will be your guide for laying your subbase and slabs at the correct fall.

06

Compact the subbase

Next, compact the subbase to create a solid foundation. For small patios and paths, a hand tamper can work (see p.69), but most projects benefit from a power compactor, which you can rent from a local rental company.

Compact the subbase with overlapping passes, covering the surface three or four times. Add more crushed stone if you notice any spots dropping below your marks on the wooden pegs. Then compact again until you have an even, solid base.

07

Lay the mortar bed

Start by mixing a bedding mortar of 1:4 cement and sharp sand. Lay a mortar bed in one corner for the first slab around 1½ in (40 mm) thick, using a trowel to spread enough to cover the entire slab area. The mix should be moist but not so wet that the slabs sink.

Tip

For larger patios, ordering crushed limestone in bulk bags or by truckload from a builders' merchant is much more cost effective.

08

Apply primer

Using a brush or builder's trowel, apply a primer (such as an SBR primer) to the back of each slab before laying it, making sure the entire slab is covered. This will ensure a strong bond with the mortar bed and will vastly improve the longevity of your patio.

USING SPACERS

For a contemporary stone like porcelain or a sawed natural stone, you can use spacers for consistent joints. A ¼-in (5-mm) gap, or wider if preferred, will give a clean, uniform finish to the patio. It will also make positioning easier for the next slab. For every slab you lay, add your spacers in.

09

Lay the first slab

Position the first slab carefully on the bed at one corner and ensure it has full contact with the mortar bed. Lay the first slab so it's level at one edge and slopes in one direction according to the desired fall. Use the offset bubble on your level as a guide for the fall (see p.61). If you are using a string line, follow the string line to guide the fall. Tap the slab into place with a rubber mallet until it's level and aligned. The first slab is crucial, so take your time to get it just right.

You can then replicate the fall across the rest of your slabs as you move through the first row, using either the offset bubble or the string line.

10

Lay the remaining slabs

Once the first slab is set, move on to the next one, following the same procedure. Continue laying the rest of the slabs. The first slab will be set at the correct fall, so simply replicate the same fall with the next slab. Keep checking that each slab is level with the others using your level. Make sure there are no gaps under your level—if there are, you will need to lift the slab and re-bed it.

Here, I'm laying a natural sandstone with rough, undulating edges. In this instance, I have to gauge the thickness of the joints (spaces between slabs) by eye because every slab is unique. I'm aiming for ½-in (10-mm) joints.

CUTTING SLABS

Often, you will need to make cuts when you start a new row of paving to create a staggered or stretcher bond (see p.57). For this, you will need to use a stone cutter such as an angle grinder. Ensure you have the right blades for cutting natural stone and wear the appropriate personal protective equipment (PPE), such as steel toecaps, glasses, gloves, and ear protectors.

APPLYING SEALER

You can apply a natural stone sealer to protect the patio from the elements and staining. It's best to do this on a dry day with consecutive dry days forecast to allow ample time for the sealer to cure. You can apply it either after installation or before you lay the slabs. Some stone suppliers offer a pre-sealing service, which can be very helpful, especially when you have plenty of other tasks to focus your energy on.

11

Prepare for pointing

Allow the mortar to set for at least 24–48 hours. Make sure the patio is dry and you have two consecutive days of dry weather before you start your pointing—rain will cause a mess, stain the slabs, and compromise the structural integrity of your jointing compound. Sweep and clean the area to prepare for pointing.

12

Fill and smooth the joints

There are various pointing options, but a simple sand and cement mix or kiln-dried sand for flexible joints works well. For this patio, I used a 1:4 mix of cement and building sand. The mix is wet enough so it clumps together when you squeeze it, but not too wet that it's a nightmare to work with and stains the slabs. Using a small trowel, start filling the joints, ensuring you push enough mortar into each joint—it's best to overfill.

After you've filled the joints, use a pointing iron to smooth over the filled joints. This will give you a nice smooth finish to your patio.

13

Finish off

Once you've finished the pointing, sweep the excess mortar away.

A beautiful, natural stone patio creates a lovely space to relax and enjoy the garden.

How long it takes at least 2 weekends **Best time to do** spring, summer, or fall

Project
How to build a rustic brick path

Here, we'll look at how to build an extremely tough, durable brick path that can handle regular wheelbarrow traffic. The method for setting out and constructing a path is often quite similar to building a patio, especially if you're opting for a more durable surface.

Before you start

You need to decide exactly where you want your path to go and how wide it will be. A comfortable path width is between 3 and 4 ft (0.9 and 1.2 m). Here, I'm installing a path that will be approximately 4 ft (1.2 m) wide. When you excavate the site, you should allow for at least 4 in (100 mm) of subbase material, a mortar bed of between ¾ and 1¾ in (20 and 30 mm), and the depth of the brick. See p.54 for information on calculating the amount of subbase you'll need.

First, mark the area where your path will go. For a straight, linear path, I like to use iron pins and a string line to mark the length and width of the path. For curved paths, you can use an old hose to shape the curves.

MATERIALS

- Geotextile membrane
- Crushed limestone for the subbase
- Sharp sand
- Cement
- Frost-proof bricks
- SBR primer (optional)
- Building sand
- Kiln-dried sand (optional)

TOOLS

- String line and iron pins (or hose)
- Lump hammer
- Tape measure
- Spray paint
- Spade
- Hand tamper or power compactor
- Brick bolster or angle grinder and PPE (goggles, ear protectors, gloves, mask, and steel toecaps)
- Rubber mallet
- Boat level
- Builder's trowel
- Builder's square
- Long level
- Soft brush
- Pointing trowel
- Pointing iron

01

Mark out the site

For straight paths, hammer in pins at the beginning and end point of your path. Attach a string line to the two pins to create a straight edge. Then measure the width of your path across from each pin and add a string line parallel to the first one. Use spray paint to spray along the lines to create your area for excavation. For curved paths, you can use a hose to outline the path and spray along the outline.

02

Excavate the site

With your path marked out, dig the area to the required depth for at least 4 in (100 mm) of subbase material, a mortar bed of between ¾ and 1¾ in (20 and 30 mm), and the depth of the chosen finish—in this case, a brick's depth.

03

Prepare the base

Next, lay and install a geotextile membrane cut to the appropriate size of your space. It will stop your subbase material from combining and mixing in with the soil beneath.

Insert pegs every 3 ft (1 m) along the path to guide the finished height of your subbase.

SLOPED PATHS

For a sloped path, follow the natural gradient of the slope and keep the relative depth level. The key is to work with the slope so the path blends into the landscape. If the gradient is steep—anything greater than a 1:12 fall—it's worth considering tiering the path and integrating a step or two.

04

Lay the subbase

Next, lay your subbase. Crushed limestone is the most common subbase material. Compact it with a hand tamper or power compactor. Since this is a relatively small section of path, I am using a hand tamper.

05

Set out the edges

Always start with the edges. Set up your level string lines to guide the placement of your edging. For edging, I use a strong mortar mix of 1:4 cement to sharp sand—the same mix I recommend for slab paving, because it's crucial the edges of your path are solid. You can slurry the underside of the bricks with primer for added strength and longevity.

Tip

Start the path with a row of full bricks before you make your half-brick cut for the next row so you won't have any awkward cuts to navigate.

06

Lay the edge bricks

Lay the bricks on a bed of mortar, tapping them down so they sit level with the string line. Use a small boat level to make sure the individual bricks are level along the length and width of the brick. You can leave space for a joint if you prefer, or you can butt them up—it depends on the look you want to achieve.

07

Haunch the sides

Haunch the outer sides, creating a ridge or angled bed of cement using your trowel to really secure those edges in place.

08

Cut away excess mortar

Cut away any excess mortar on the inside edges with a trowel so it doesn't impact laying the infill bricks. Before starting with the infill, complete the edging on both sides and leave it to set for 24–48 hours.

09

Cut your half bricks

Before you start infilling the path, measure and cut your half bricks required for the alternate rows. You can use a brick bolster or angle grinder for cutting. An angle grinder gives a cleaner finish, but be sure to wear goggles, ear protectors, a mask, and steel toecaps when cutting.

10

Infill the path

Now you can start laying the bricks. Here I'm using a stretcher bond (see p.57). Lay a mortar bed of the same mortar mix and place your bricks into position. Use a builder's square to ensure the bricks are set out at a 90-degree angle from the edges.

MORTAR BED

Since this path will see heavy foot traffic, I laid the bricks on a full mortar bed for added strength. I used the same mortar mix—1:4 cement and sharp sand. For a less hard-wearing path, you could just use a bed of sharp sand.

11

Check the levels

After each row, tap down the bricks with a rubber mallet and use a level to ensure they're flush with the edges. There should be no gaps underneath the level. I've left generous joints between the bricks for a pronounced look and for ease of pointing, but you can butt them up together if you prefer. Judge the joints by eye or use a finger's thickness. Continue filling the path.

12

Point the joints

Allow the mortar to set for at least 24–48 hours. Make sure the path is dry and you have two consecutive days of dry weather before you start your pointing.

There are various ways to point a path depending on the size of joints you have chosen. For small joints where the bricks are butted together, kiln-dried sand would be your best option. Just split open a bag and sweep it into the gaps with a soft brush. Because this path is laid on a solid mortar bed, I'm using a 1:4 pointing mix of cement and building sand.

Sweep and clean the area to prepare for pointing. Using a small trowel, start filling the joints, ensuring you push enough mortar into each joint—it's best to overfill.

13

Smooth the joints

After you've filled the joints, use a pointing iron to smooth over the filled joints to give you a nice, smooth finish to your path. Once you've finished the pointing, sweep the excess mortar away.

And there we have the beginnings of a traditional brick path, offering a timeless look and feel.

Steps

Steps are often a way to cater to level changes in a yard, based on the topography of the space. However, steps can provide so much more than just a transition between levels—they can be designed for their aesthetic appeal and to control the pace at which people experience and move around spaces. In this section, I'll show you how to build steps.

A set of rustic brick steps echoes the traditional nature of this town garden in Sussex.

Shape, style, and size

Steps come in a wide array of different shapes, styles, and sizes. You can get creative with the materials and the overall visual aesthetic, such as traditional brick steps or ones made from rustic railroad ties. Staggered floating concrete steps create a contemporary look, or you can use steel steps for an industrial vibe.

The possibilities are limitless, so decide on a style that works for your space and is practical for the people who will use the steps. If elderly people or young children, maybe even pets, will use the space, you'll need wide, comfortable steps that are accessible to all. Steep, narrow steps are a challenge for those who are less mobile. I aim for a minimum step width of 3 ft (1 m).

Ramps

Ramps are useful if a space going to be used by people with limited mobility or wheelchair users, or to get strollers or wheelbarrows from A to B. The gradient of a ramp should be no steeper than 1:12 for ease of use. Choose your materials to suit the environment and aesthetic design, and opt for a slip-resistant material to prevent any falls.

How long it takes 2 weekends **Best time to do** spring, summer, or fall

Project
How to build block and brick steps

Here, we'll look at building steps using concrete blocks and a brick fascia. Note that I'm recessing the steps into a bank, so the steps will be framed with a retaining block wall to keep the earth around them. This is quite a common way to build steps, but, of course, there are many alternatives that could be applicable to your project.

Calculate your steps

Measure the height from the ground level (bottom of bottom step) to the top (top of top step). Then you'll need to calculate the number of steps required for a comfortable transition between the two levels. You will also need to calculate the optimum tread depth of your steps based on the horizontal length of the set of steps.

This is where you will need to apply some simple math. I recommend a comfortable step height (riser) of between 5½ and 6¾ in (140 and 170 mm) and a comfortable tread depth of between 10 and 18 in (250 and 450 mm). Anything less or more can become an awkward trip hazard. Use this range to calculate the quantity of steps needed with a comfortable riser and tread. Also try to ensure all of your risers and treads are of equal size for ease of use.

Make sure you factor in the width of your joints when you calculate materials.

MATERIALS

- Crushed limestone
- Cement
- Ballast
- Building sand
- Concrete blocks: 17 x 8½ x 4 in (440 x 215 x 100 mm)
- Wall ties
- Brick pavers: 8 x 4 x 2 in (200 x 100 x 50 mm)

TOOLS

- String line and iron pins
- Builder's square
- Spade or pickax
- Wooden pegs
- Lump hammer
- Spirit level
- Cement mixer or wheelbarrow
- Rake
- Builder's trowel
- Pointing iron
- Brush

Set out the site

Using pins and string line, measure and mark out the overall length and width of your steps on the ground. Allow an extra 12 in (300 mm) on each measurement to spread the weight. It will allow the blockwork to sit comfortably on the foundation rather than the edge, which would create too much pressure and potentially cause your foundation to fail. Use the 3:4:5 method (see p.59) or a builder's square to ensure corners are square.

Steps cross-section
This cross-section of a set of steps highlights all of the key components, including the total length and height of the steps and individual riser and tread measurements.

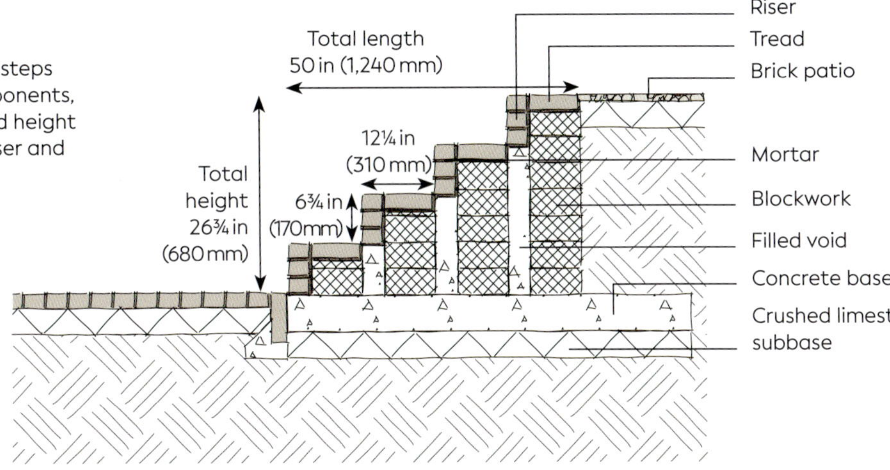

01

Excavate the site

Dig out the entire space to a minimum of 10 in (250 mm) below the bottom step. In most yards, you will need a subbase of 4 in (100 mm) of crushed limestone and 6 in (150 mm) poured concrete on top, but if your yard is on flint or chalk, you can just lay concrete for your step foundations.

02

Set your levels

Insert wooden pegs into the ground as your guidance for your subbase levels—your finished height should allow for both the stone and poured concrete. Use a level to determine the height of your pegs relative to the landing point—the top of your peg should be level with the floor height.

Bang in pegs at intervals, making sure all of the tops are level with each other. This gives you a great marker and framework for installing a level subbase. If you're installing the 4 in (100 mm) of crushed stone, mark a point on each of the pegs to guide where to layer it up to before pouring the concrete.

03

Lay the foundations

Here I'm forgoing the 4in (100mm) of subbase. Mix your concrete to a 1:5 ratio of cement and ballast. Pour it, use a rake to distribute it, and then tamp it down, using the pegs as your reference point. You can use the bottom of a level or plank of wood for this part, but you'll have to clean your level afterward, so you may wish to avoid the mess!

Remove the wooden pegs and leave your foundation to cure for 48 hours before building your block wall and steps.

04

Lay the blocks in a U shape

Mix your mortar to a 1:4 ratio of cement and building sand. Start by laying the outer perimeter of blocks for the length and width of your steps on a bed of mortar. You may need to cut some to size at the ends. This will create a U-shaped structure, which is the framework for your steps. Make sure your blocks are level horizontally and vertically. Lay the blocks to a string line for complete accuracy, and ensure your corners are square using a builder's square or the 3:4:5 method (see p.59).

05

Do a dry run

Once you have completed the U shape, it's time to do a dry run of blocks and bricks to make sure your steps work out in accordance with your calculations. It's important to do a dry run of all materials, blocks, and the brick face so you know exactly what your tread depths will be. Also allow for the joints. For standard brick and concrete blockwork, this is about ½in (10mm).

Once you are happy, make a mark on the bottom tier of blocks where each of your steps will start.

06

Finish the block wall

Continue building up the U-shaped block wall on a bed of mortar to the finished height of the steps, checking it's horizontally and vertically level during every step of the process.

Where there will be an adjoining step set, insert a wall tie into the mortar for every course of blocks so that all of the brick steps are tied into the blockwork walls.

Wall ties

07

Lay the first block steps

To create the block steps, lay a row of horizontal blocks on a bed of mortar where your markers are, allowing for the width of the brick face in front of it.

Repeat the process for each step, laying blocks behind the last row to create the step riser. Keep checking the levels while working through the rest of the blockwork.

08

Fill the voids

You then need to fill the voids behind the blocks with rubble or crushed limestone. To prevent any future subsidence, you can cap it with 4 in (100 mm) of concrete, but it's not essential. If you use concrete, you'll need to wait 24–48 hours for the concrete to cure before proceeding to the next step.

09

Face the blockwork

Lay your brick riser on a mortar bed (the same mix) nice and tight to the face of each concrete block riser. Ensure there is consistency with your jointing gap between each brick—½ in (10 mm) is your guide. For the second step, lay your brick riser on the filled void

11

Joint the bricks

Use a pointing iron to joint the brickwork with a 1:4 mix of cement and building sand. Start with the vertical joints and then the horizontals.

10

Finish the risers

Repeat this process until all of the risers are covered and to the required height. Your finished brick riser height should be level or proud of the blockwork. In this instance, I'm using bricks as the treads, so I've made the brick risers higher than the blockwork so the tread bricks can sit flush behind the facing brickwork.

12

Finish the treads

You can be creative with laying the bricks for the treads. Apply a mortar bed and start laying your treads in your chosen format. Repeat this process until all of your treads are complete.

13

Point and allow to cure

To match the brick face of the riser, point the step treads using a 1:4 mix of cement and building sand. Ideally, avoid using your steps for at least 48 hours so the mortar and concrete can fully cure before any footfall. Once cured, brush down the steps and rinse off any remaining dust or mortar residue. You can render the inside walls or face them with brickwork. Make sure you account for this depth when calculating the width of your steps.

This set of rustic brick steps with a detailed finish and rendered wall draws the eye into the space beyond.

Retaining and garden walls

Walls are permanent structures and can serve multiple purposes. Retaining walls are commonly used to retain earth, cater for level changes and slopes, or define a particular section of the yard, such as a patio or seating area. Garden walls, such as single-skin walls (one layer of bricks), provide decorative detail and definition. In this section, I'll show you how to build a retaining wall.

Walls in landscaping

From a design perspective, retaining and garden walls can be used in many ways. They offer vertical interest to any outside space and can be used to enhance the visual interest of your yard. Retaining walls can provide structural support to manage a slope or to create level terraces on a slope.

Given that brickwork retains heat, walls can also provide microclimates (see p.16) for plants, such as tender plants next to a south-facing wall. You can use walls to create stunning backdrops for beautiful planting plans, to define zones in a garden, and to create integrated seating or dining areas.

Different construction formations produce a particular look and feel. Long, straight walls emphasize the length of a space and create the illusion of a yard being bigger that it actually is. Curved walls can redefine the shape of an existing space and create a dynamic atmosphere. Staggered walls cutting in horizontally break up the space, creating width and visual interest.

Opposite A wall can create a microclimate that is perfect for certain plants, such as a warm spot from heat radiating from a south-facing wall.

Material choices

Material options vary massively, from old railroad ties and natural stone and brick to steel and render. It's important to think about your material choices in alignment with other hard landscaping choices in the garden and your surroundings. Matching building materials to the existing facade of the house or to the stone in the local area creates a strong, more cohesive design.

GARDEN SCREENING

Garden screening is a less permanent option to define spaces or disguise certain views. A lighter-weight screen isn't suitable to retain large quantities of earth, but you could use screening in a variety of ways to create the impression of a wall and divider between areas. It can be a simple trellis or Corten steel panels in the middle of a border—there are many possible solutions on the market, and you can create a great effect by mixing up your materials.

How long it takes 2 weekends **Best time to do** spring, summer, or fall

Project
How to build a retaining wall

Here, we will build a retaining wall using concrete blocks with a brick-face finish. You could also use render or cladding for the finish. This project will allow you to practice both blockwork and brickwork, two skills that you can then apply in a multitude of different projects.

The blockwork method

One of the first landscaping skills I learned was building a block retaining wall faced with brick for the new patio we installed. It was one of the most satisfying jobs of the project because of the instant impact it created. It was only around 2 ft (60 cm) high and faced with brick, but it clearly defined the shape and outline of the patio.

Laying blockwork is relatively straightforward, and it's a great place to start and build confidence with your landscaping skills before moving into more intricate bricklaying. The retaining wall in this project is a three-sided U shape that forms the framework for steps. See p.54 for information on calculating materials.

If you're planning to build a retaining wall more than 4 ft (1.2 m) high, it's advisable to seek the services of a fully qualified structural engineer. They will be able to assess the ground conditions and soil mechanics before construction.

MATERIALS

- Crushed limestone for the subbase
- Cement
- Ballast
- Building sand
- Concrete blocks: 17 x 8½ x 4 in (440 x 215 x 100 mm)
- Plastic pipe: 1½ in (40 mm) diameter
- Wall ties
- Frost-proof bricks
- Bitumen, tar, or damp-proof membrane (optional)
- Gravel or crushed stone
- Coping stones (optional)
- Render (optional)

TOOLS

- Tape measure
- String line and iron pins
- Builder's square
- Spade or mattock
- Wooden pegs
- Lump hammer
- Spirit level
- Piece of timber (optional)
- Hand tamper
- Cement mixer or wheelbarrow
- Rake
- Angle grinder and PPE (goggles, ear protectors, gloves, mask, and steel toecaps)
- Builder's trowel
- Pointing iron
- Brush

Wall cross-section
Concrete blocks on a concrete foundation form the framework for the wall, which has a brick-face finish.

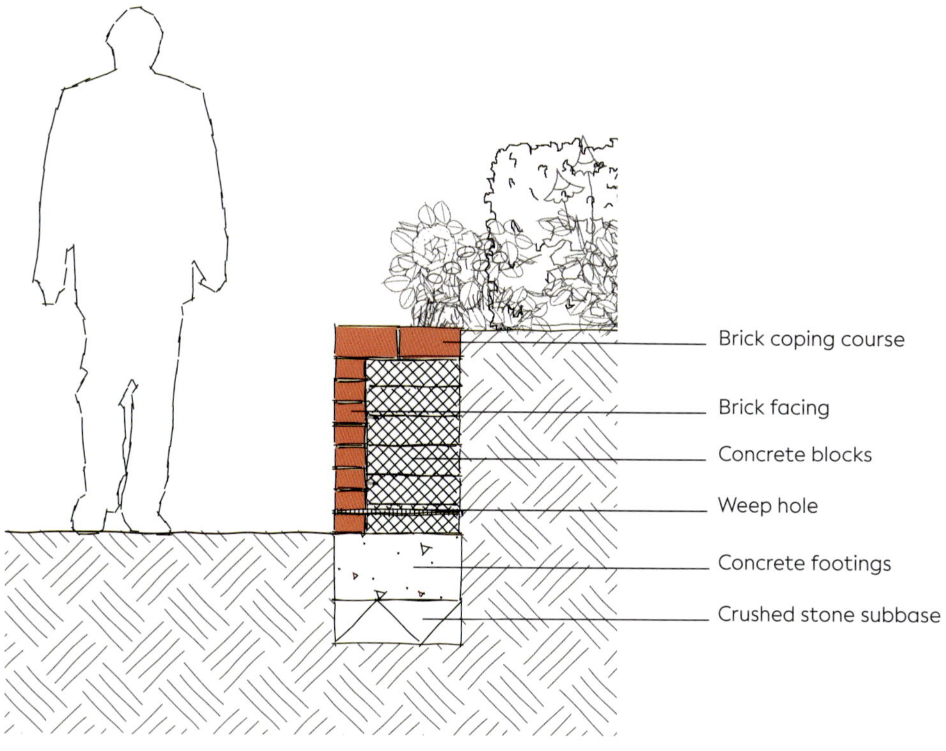

Tip

For walls higher than 3 ft (1 m), you may need a mini digger and a concrete pour and pump (see p.45). For smaller walls, you can dig and mix concrete by hand.

01

Dig the footings

Clear the site, removing any obstacles so the area is clear and ready to build on. Measure and mark exactly where your retaining wall will go. Use string lines as a guide to create a straight, defined line and a builder's square to make sure corners are square.

You'll need to dig deep enough to support the wall's weight. For a wall under 4 ft (1.2 m) high, the depth is typically between 12 and 18 in (300 and 450 mm) and at least twice the width of the blocks. Plan to lay a solid 6 in (150 mm) of crushed limestone compacted at the bottom of the trench.

02

Set the levels

Insert wooden pegs at even spacings to set the height for the base of the retaining wall. Check they're level with a spirit level. This will help as a guide for laying your crushed stone layer and concrete. Clear away the excess soil from the site to keep your workspace open.

If you're building on soft ground, spread and lay your subbase layer of stone now, using a hand tamper to compact it down. I'm building on solid ground, so I'm skipping the stone layer

03

Pour the concrete footing

Use a concrete mix of 1:5 cement and ballast. Pour the concrete into the trench and rake it over until you've reached the height of your wooden marker pegs.

04

Tamp the concrete

Use a level or straight piece of timber to tamp down the concrete to create a completely level surface. Allow the concrete to cure for at least 48 hours before moving on to the blockwork.

05

Lay the first row of blocks

Set up a level string line at the height of the blocks as a guide, and lay a ¾-in (20-mm) mortar bed of 1:4 cement and building sand. Lay the first row of blocks on top. Spread the end of each block with mortar to create a ½-in (10-mm) joint. For a more solid wall, lay your blocks flat on their wider side. Check they are level horizontally and vertically.

For the next course, stagger the blocks to create a stretcher bond (see p.57).

06

Insert the pipe

Every 3 ft (1 m) or so horizontally, leave a 2-in (50-mm) gap between the blocks to allow for the drainage pipe (known as a weep hole). If water builds up behind the wall, it will flow through the pipe and out the front of the wall. Insert a cut-to-size plastic pipe at least one course of blocks above ground level in the 2-in (50-mm) gap. The pipe will later be covered by and sit flush with the finished surface layer (in this case, bricks), so allow for the depth of the finished surface.

07

Build the blockwork

Continue adding layers of blockwork, checking for alignment as you go—always use your level to check the blocks are vertically plumb.

Note that you can backfill the wall as you build to make the process easier (see step 9).

08

Insert the wall ties and point the joints

Every 24 in (600 mm) horizontally, add a wall tie while the mortar joints are still wet. For added strength, stagger the ties vertically between courses. If you're working over consecutive days, be sure to insert ties at the end of each day's work, or you'll have to add them later by drilling into the dry mortar.

As the mortar dries, use a pointing iron to finish the joints, smoothing the verticals first and then the horizontals.

09

Backfill the wall

Use gravel or crushed stone as a drainage layer for the first 12 in (300 mm) behind the wall, which will allow water to filter through and escape through the drainage pipes. Then continue backfilling with crushed stone, rubble, or soil on top of your drainage layer.

For extra protection, you can seal the back of the block wall with bitumen or tar or lay damp-proof membrane, which will prevent excess water from seeping in.

10

Face the block wall

There are many options for facing your block wall. You could lay a brick face, add render to the wall for a smooth, contemporary finish, or use steel or timber cladding.

To lay a brick face, use the block wall as a guide and lay bricks to a string line in exactly the same way as you did with the blocks. Use a trowel to lay an even bed of mortar, using the same mix as before.

Lay the bricks with a stretcher bond (see p.57), ensuring each layer is vertically plumb with a level. Aim for joints no thicker than ½ in (10 mm). As you lay each course, bed down the wall ties to secure the bricks to the block wall.

11

Point and add the coping

Once the mortar begins to set, use a pointing iron to finish the brickwork, moving from vertical to horizontal joints for a clean finish.

To hide the blockwork and to finish the wall, cap it with coping stones or bricks laid on edge. You have many options here, but bricks on edge provide a really attractive and traditional finish to a wall. Just ensure that when you install coping, you lay it with a slight fall to ensure water doesn't pool on top of the wall.

Once the wall is complete, give it a final brush-down to remove any loose mortar. You can add render if you wish. Then step back and marvel at the retaining wall you've just built!

This retaining wall frames steps for a change in level between spaces. The blockwork is finished with a white render and capped with bricks laid on edge.

Beds and borders

Beds and borders are the foundations for your planting and come in all shapes and sizes, from large, perennial beds to small, island beds in a new-build garden. They can be adapted to suit any setting and will help to shape and define your outside space. Here, I'll show you how to make a simple raised bed that you can complete in a few hours.

The perennial borders in my previous garden are expansive and are defined by natural logs and wood chip paths.

From ground-level beds and borders to raised beds, gardeners have become very creative over the years to maximize growing potential. I recommend that the ratio of planting to your hard landscaping, such as paved areas and paths, is 60:40 or 70:30. This will provide a more balanced look while ensuring you have a thriving ecosystem for birds and beneficial wildlife to enjoy and inhabit. That said, gardens are a personal preference, and some people may prefer the balance flipped the other way.

Edging

If you plan to have ground-level beds and borders in your garden, it's important to think about definition—that is, how the edges of your borders and beds are defined and what materials are used to edge them.

There's a wide variety of options available, from plastic lawn edging and Corten steel to rustic brick and timber edging. Select an edging material that neatly defines your planting spaces while adding to the character and charm. Consider longevity and look and feel. While timber suits a naturalistic garden, be mindful that it will start to rot after a few years.

Ground preparation

Dig out new ground-level beds to a minimum of 12 in (300 mm) deep. Break up and till the substrate by a further 6–12 in (150–300 mm). This will allow the new topsoil and/or compost to work itself into the subsoil below, helping to improve your soil structure and fertility over time.

Raised beds

Whether you're a vegetable-growing fanatic or someone who loves growing flowers for cutting, raised beds are hugely versatile because they allow you to grow your chosen plants in the best conditions. It's no surprise they are hugely popular with gardeners, particularly in urban gardens, where ground-level planting can be a challenge.

Raised beds can have a variety of uses. They can be used to:

- grow vegetables, fruit, and cut flowers
- provide optimum planting conditions when the garden lacks good, deep soil
- raise the height of planting to make routine maintenance more accessible
- screen out certain areas of the garden by raising the planting height
- minimize damage to planting caused by young children or pets—planting in the ground can be more susceptible to flattening from little ones and pets
- control the growing medium for plants that prefer particular soil conditions, such as acidic soil for blueberries and lingonberries.

There are many different raised bed options available on the market, and you can buy off-the-shelf products in timber or steel kits, for example. Building your own raised bed out of railroad ties or treated timber is straightforward, though, and something you could easily do during the space of a few hours on a weekend. I built six raised beds over the course of a weekend using sawed treated timber and some decking screws.

How long it takes 3–4 hours **Best time to do** spring, summer, or fall

Project
How to build a raised bed

Here, I'll show you how to build a basic raised bed using treated boards from a local woodyard. You could use thicker boards or railroad ties to suit your style, and you can adjust the size as needed based on your preferences.

Calculate the size

First, figure out the size of your raised bed. If the bed is too wide, it will be hard to reach the middle from either side, so choose a width you can comfortably work with. The one I'm building is 4 ft (1.2 m) wide. The length also impacts the need for support posts in the middle—for a 6-ft- (1.8-m-) long bed, four corner posts should do just fine.

The height of your raised bed is down to personal preferences, where it's situated, and what you intend to grow. For example, if you site your raised bed on hard ground with no earth beneath, you will want a decent depth to your raised bed so the plants can gather enough nutrients and goodness from the contained soil. If you're growing certain vegetables, such as long-rooted carrots, they require soil with a decent depth.

Once you have your dimensions, cut the timber boards to fit the length and width of your planned bed. The height of the bed will determine how many layers you need, so cut enough boards to reach your desired height.

MATERIALS

- Treated timber posts: 3 x 3 in (75 x 75 mm)
- Half bag concrete mix per post
- Treated boards: 6 x 1½ in (150 x 38 mm)
- Timber decking screws: 3 x ⅛ in (75 x 4.5 mm)
- Old plastic bags
- Felting nails
- Logs or woody twigs (optional)
- Well-rotted manure (optional)
- Compost
- Topsoil

TOOLS

- Tape measure
- String line and iron pins
- Builder's square
- Post hole digger
- Drill or screwdriver
- Hand saw or circular saw
- Hammer
- Wheelbarrow

01

Set out and prepare the ground

Mark out the bed's perimeter with string lines and pins to the size you need. Make sure it's square by measuring diagonally between corners with a builder's square or use the 3:4:5 method (see p.59).

Once your string line is set and level, do some ground prep to even things out, although you can make further adjustments when attaching the boards to the posts.

02

Dig the holes for the corner posts

With your string line as a guide, dig holes in each corner for the posts. This isn't a heavy-duty structure, so you need only to dig each hole to about 12 in (300 mm) deep.

If you're adding a bed on top of concrete or compacted soil, there's no need to dig the posts in—you'll create a standalone structure.

03

Set the posts

Set the posts in using concrete mix, ensuring they're vertically level and square with the string line. Position the posts in the hole and pour half a bag of concrete mix into the hole until it has almost reached the surface. Fill the hole up with water until the water spills over the top. Leave it to set for 20 minutes. Leave the posts slightly taller than the final raised bed height.

04

Secure the boards

Now build the sides. Pre-drill the holes to stop the wood from splitting. Use timber decking screws to attach the boards to each corner post. Start at the bottom and work in layers until you've reached your desired bed height. Cut down the corner posts flush to the boards if you wish, or leave for a more pronounced look.

06

Fill the bed

How you fill the bed depends on its height. For a deep bed, such as 24 in (600 mm) high, consider filling the lower section with logs or woody material, which will break down naturally over time, to save on cost. Then top up with compost and topsoil. For a standard-size bed, such as 12 in (300 mm) high, add a generous amount of well-rotted manure to the base of the bed to enhance soil structure and then top up with topsoil and compost.

And that's it—you now have a raised bed ready for planting.

05

Line the bed

Lining will provide an extra layer of protection to the wood, stopping moisture from sitting next to it and so increasing longevity. This is a good way to repurpose old plastic bags. Cut your bags to size and secure them to the inside of your raised bed using a hammer and felting nails.

I've added a hazel lattice (see pp.110–113) to my raised bed, where I'm growing delphiniums and other ornamental plants.

Outdoor structures

Outdoor structures, such as a pergola or arch, can add great vertical interest, providing a stunning walkway or defining seating and entertainment areas. They also double up as perfect companions for growing climbing plants.

Structures in landscape design

Outdoor structures are generally permanent features, so when everything else starts to fade throughout the year, they come into their own. Structures can be used to elevate the design and set the mood and overall tone of a space. For example, installing a large, archetypal Roman arch creates a historical, traditional theme.

Structures can be used as destination points, such as a greenhouse with a path leading to it. They can also act as standalone focal points or as a frame to a focal point. My pergola, for instance, is a standalone focal point at the end of a path, encouraging people to investigate and explore different zones of the garden.

You don't need to include an abundance of structures to have a great impact—sometimes too much can create a feeling of chaos, especially if the structures are all different heights. Less is definitely more, so think about where a vertical structure could be added—perhaps to create a shaded seating area, to provide support for climbing plants, or to connect different areas throughout the space.

Remember that if you plant deciduous climbers around the structure, it will be bare for a large part of the year, so make sure you're happy with its bare aesthetic.

Material choices

It's important to think about the material choices that will suit your space. Pergolas and arches, for example, can be constructed from timber, metal, or natural stone, or a combination of the three. You can either match materials and colors to the overall style and aesthetic of your house and yard, for instance, or choose ones that contrast. Although separate from the house, structures need to work seamlessly with it in the space.

How long it takes 1 weekend **Best time to do** spring, summer, or fall

Project
How to build a pergola

Here, we will look at a step-by-step project for building a wooden pergola. We will be using some of the same principles and techniques we employed for fencing (see pp.48–51) to complete the structure.

A pergola can be used in a variety of settings. It adds something a little different stylistically to a garden, while providing a functional space to enjoy throughout the year.

MATERIALS

4 treated timber posts: $7\frac{3}{4}$ft x 6in x 6in (2.4m x 150mm x 150mm)

4 bags concrete mix

Sleeper screws: 6 x $\frac{1}{4}$in (150 x 6.7mm)

Timber screws: 3 x $\frac{1}{8}$in (75 x 4.5mm)

4 treated timber front and side bearers: 10ft x 6in x 2in (3m x 150mm x 50mm)

Galvanized steel corners (optional)

2 treated timber roof beam fixings: $7\frac{3}{4}$ft x 2in x 2in (2.4m x 50mm x 50mm)

6 treated timber roof beams: $7\frac{3}{4}$ft x 3in x 3in (2.4m x 75mm x 75mm)

Wood preserver or paint

TOOLS

Tape measure

String line and iron pins

Builder's square

Post hole digger

Spirit level

Hand saw or circular saw

Drill or screwdriver

Miter saw (optional)

Pencil

01

Mark out the post holes

Start by marking out where each corner post will go using pins and a string line. The pergola I'm building here is 9 x 7½ ft (2.8 x 2.3 m). The corners should be completely square, so measure corner to corner with a builder's square or use the 3:4:5 method (see p.59).

02

Dig the post holes

Use a post hole digger to start digging the holes for the posts. Here, I'm using 6 x 6 in (150 x 150 mm) posts, so the holes need to be twice the diameter of the post and at least 24 in (600 mm) deep.

03

Position and level the first post

Place your first post in one of the holes, ensuring it's vertically straight and lined up with your string line.

04

Concrete the first post

Set the post in using one bag of concrete mix and let cure for at least 20 minutes.

05

Position and concrete the second post

Position your next post and ensure the two posts are level with each other. Screw one end of a length of timber to the fixed post as a temporary guide and attach the other end to the second post. Use a level on top to check that they're aligned. If not, add or remove a little soil around the second post until they sit level.

Set the second post in using concrete mix in the same way, ensuring that it's vertically straight. Repeat this process for all the corner posts.

06

Install the front, rear, and side bearers

Use a saw to cut down your four bearers for the front, rear, and sides so they sit flush with the outside edge of each post. Check using a level before screwing in place. Pre-drill the holes to avoid the wood splitting. Then fix the bearers to the central part of the main upright post using 6 x ¼in (150 x 6.7 mm) sleeper screws. Repeat this process until your four main sides are complete.

If you want a seamless finish, you can use a miter saw to cut the end of your bearers at a 45-degree angle, but it's not essential. Alternatively, you can add galvanized steel corners for a neat look.

07

Install roof beam fixings

Once the bearers are in place, it's time to install the roof beam fixings. Use 3 x ⅛in (75 x 4.5 mm) timber screws to affix a length of 2 x 2 in (50 x 50 mm) treated timber, cut to the size of your structure, 1 in (25 mm) above the lower edge of the front and rear bearers. This will be your fixing point for the roof beams.

Tip

If you're building by yourself, you'll need to use something to prop up the end of the roof beams while you position and screw them in place.

08

Measure and cut the roof beams

Measure from the inside edge of the front and rear bearers and cut your roof beams to the required length. If your pergola is square, you can cut one to the correct length and use it as a template for the others.

09

Space the roof beams

With a tape measure and pencil, mark on the front and rear bearers where your roof beams will go to create even gaps between them. Divide the length of the bearers by the number of roof beams, taking into account the beams' width, to give you the correct spacing for each bearer. If you want to create more shade, opt for more roof beams to create a slatted look.

10

Fix the roof beams

Pre-drill the holes. Using a 3 x ⅛in (75 x 4.5mm) timber screw, affix the first roof beam to the front and rear roof beam fixings from underneath and angled upward. Repeat this process until all of your roof beams are in place.

If a roof beam needs replacing in the future, you can just zip the screws out, remove the beam, and affix a new one in place.

FINISH AND SEAL

Once the structure is complete, you could give it a coat of paint or a clear wood preserver to protect it from the elements. If you're planning to grow climbing plants, add your plant supports now. You can install sturdy wires for growing roses or trellises down the sides of the structure. To give the pergola some extra detail, you can attach cast-iron brackets on the corners, which are perfect for hanging baskets.

Outdoor seating

A yard wouldn't be complete without somewhere to sit! From benches and dining tables to loungers and sofas, outdoor seating is a must-have for any outside space. After all the hard work you've put into building and nurturing your space, you need that perfect spot to sit back and relax, admiring all of the fruits of your labor.

The layout you've chosen for your space and its aspect (see pp.14–15) will somewhat determine where your entertainment and seating areas are. Choose places for seating based on your preferences—where can you enjoy the morning sun with a cup of coffee? Where can you soak up the last of the evening sun? Where are the spots with dappled shade to enjoy the best of both worlds? What vistas look particularly appealing throughout the day? Also consider the practicalities, such as positioning dining areas near the house for ease of access.

With these areas defined, it's now time to go shopping, and given the large array of outdoor furniture and different styles out there, this is where you can really jazz things up and start to express your personality. Let's explore some classic options you may consider for your outside space.

Sofas

Outdoor sofas allow you to incorporate home comforts in your outside space, creating a lovely spot for putting your feet up, reading a book, and soaking up the ambience. They are perfect pushed up against a wall, helping to maximize space.

The style and material choices are vast, from homemade, pallet-style sofas to classy, powder-coated options, with a range of prices to match. Corner sofas are a popular choice, ideal for laid-back and casual gatherings for family and friends.

Dining tables and chairs

Dining tables and chairs will most likely be your biggest investment in outdoor seating. They can often be a statement feature, and the world's your oyster when it comes to selecting the right dining set for your outside space. Style is, of course, a key consideration, but comfort and practicality should be too—you may be using dining areas for long periods of time. Try them out first in furniture showrooms or garden centers before you commit to your purchase.

Balance and proportion are also key. There needs to be the right balance of space in and around dining furniture, making it a comfortable space to pull chairs out from underneath the table and to relax without falling off the edge of the patio. Choose a dining set that fits proportionately within the space. If your patio is relatively small, for example, a bistro set could work well.

The range of furniture in this category is extensive, from powder-coated aluminum furniture to solid, hardwood statement pieces. If you want a more modular, contemporary look, you could go for a rattan-style cube set. They come in all sizes for large and small patios, and the chairs store away nicely underneath the table, saving on space.

Benches

For me, benches are not primary seating areas—they are little spots with a lovely vista, perhaps to a focal point, or massed with planting where you can simply sit, take in your surroundings, unwind, and take a moment of calm. I like to dot benches around a space, so there's always a spot to pause and take in the surroundings.

Benches are relatively inexpensive. They come in various styles, from classic hardwood benches for a formal look to powder-coated metal benches for a contemporary look, and the prices vary. You can buy premade, off-the-shelf products, or simply build a rustic bench for the price of a few railroad ties, like the one in my garden.

Right, from top A corner sofa nestled among planting makes for a lovely spot for casual entertaining. The classic bistro set is a great option for smaller spaces and courtyards. A rustic oak sleeper bench is situated among borders to provide a tranquil resting place.

Lighting

Lighting will bring your space to life during the evenings, allowing you to enjoy your yard longer. A well-lit space can create a picturesque ambience, while a poorly lit one can be garish and make you feel like you've arrived at a football stadium.

Less is most definitely more when it comes to lighting. You should look to enhance features and create an atmospheric mood rather than installing bold and bright lighting everywhere.

Choose the right light

When choosing external lighting for your project, ensure you seek out quality equipment with an appropriate rating for external use. Lighting and other electrical equipment will be marked "suitable for outdoor use" or similar. Equipment not labeled in this way should never be used.

If you buy cheap lighting, you will end up replacing lights all too frequently. Spend a bit more to buy quality lighting that's designed to last.

With any electrical work, I always advise you to seek the services of a qualified electrician. This isn't an area you should undertake yourself, for health and safety reasons, unless, of course, you are qualified.

Lighting categories

These are the main categories of lighting for you to consider when designing and building your space.

Security lighting

Typically, motion-sensor floodlighting falls into this category, illuminating movement in dark spaces to alert you to any intruders. These lights should be placed around key entrances and exposed areas. The only downside to security lighting is that the sensors can't distinguish between wildlife and people, so your lights may be triggered at any point, causing false alarm to those at home.

Access lighting

Access lighting illuminates key access points to the property, such as entrances and paths, at night. This ensures that key paths and steps are easily accessible and straightforward to navigate in the dark.

Feature lighting

Feature lighting brings to life and enhances key features, such as an uplight on a beautiful tree or a downlight on an intricate piece of stonework. It's designed to draw your attention to core focal points.

Zonal lighting
Zonal lighting is strategically placed to light up specific zones, such as outdoor kitchens, patios, decks, and other frequently used areas.

Driveway lighting
Some lighting is specially suited for driveways and driveway entrances, including bollard and post lighting, and recessed spotlights in resin driveways.

Lighting techniques

There are a number of different lighting techniques you can use to create different effects.

Moonlighting
Moonlighting is a sophisticated method in which you attach light fittings high into trees or structures to emulate the softened light from the moon's glow.

Silhouetting
You can use lighting to silhouette objects, trees, structures, ornaments, and plants against different types of surfaces to create impressive lighting effects.

Spotlighting
Spotlighting highlights details of certain features, and is most effective when the light source is hidden from view.

Lighting temperature
Varied tones or temperatures of lighting create different atmospheres. Warm lights provide a more cozy, natural-looking vibe, while cool, bright lights give a more contemporary or modern ambience.

Downlighting
Step and path lighting highlights key walkways and steps. Downlighters can be used to cast light onto the ground, making the path or steps visible at night.

Underwater lighting
Underwater lighting, such as fountain lights, pool lights, and pond lighting, is where you can really bring water features to life at night. The movement of water or fish can create shadows, enhancing the ambience.

Below, from left Lighting techniques such as moonlighting, silhouetting, spotlighting, and downlighting create visual interest and atmosphere in an outside space.

Moonlighting

Silhouetting

Spotlighting

Downlighting

Water features

I consider water to be a vital element in any outdoor space. From a design perspective, it creates atmosphere, brings movement and visual stimulation, and instills a sense of calm. So it's no surprise many of us look to add a water feature, whether that be a formal fountain, a trickling water trough, or a pond to attract wildlife.

A Corten steel water trough planted with *Iris versicolor* captures rainwater from the greenhouse gutters. Corten is a durable material that brings a modern aesthetic to the space.

What suits your space?

Amazing effects can be created using water, from grand fountains and elegant rills flowing through a space to a simple water bowl or bubbling urn. The options are endless, so I'm confident there will be a water feature that suits your needs and the purpose of your planned space.

Your space's size and style

The size of your yard will somewhat determine what type of water feature you opt for. If you have a small space, for instance, a large fountain would look out of place, but a water trough or small pond, either in the ground or in a container, could work wonderfully.

When choosing a water feature, select a product that aligns to the style and vibe of your outside space. It should complement the garden, work with existing features, and align to the hard landscaping choices you have made for the rest of your space.

If you have decided on a formal garden with perfect symmetry, clean lines, and formal planting, for instance, a geometric water feature pre-formed from a rigid material like plastic, steel, or concrete would be ideal. This allows you to install something with precise dimensions to suit the characteristics of your garden.

Alternatively, you may have a slightly more informal setting, where using a pond to create irregular shapes would suit the design.

What do you want to achieve?

Think about what you are trying to achieve with a water feature. If you want a thriving ecosystem for wildlife, for instance, a pond is a good option. If you'd like the soothing sound of water to create a calming atmosphere, a simple water fountain or bubbling urn could be a good choice.

Installation options

It's worth checking installation before you make a purchase, because some more complex features require hard wiring and buried cables. There are many off-the-shelf products with built-in pumps and sumps, and they are usually simple to install if you have an outside power source nearby. You just plug them in and off they go, so you don't need the help of an electrician for installation. Otherwise, you will need an electrician to extend the cabling.

To hide unsightly cables, you can run them through black electrical conduit and either bury them or run them through planting beds to disguise them. Just make a note of where they are so you don't unintentionally dig them at a later point.

Choose the location

Begin by deciding exactly where to place your water feature. Consider the following:

- Power access—can you easily run power to the water feature, if needed?
- Visibility—will it be visible and accessible?
- Sunlight exposure—too much sun can encourage algae growth.
- Sound—will you benefit from the relaxing sound? Consider placing it near seating or pathways.
- Drainage—avoid areas that are prone to waterlogging.
- Safety—is it safe for kids and pets?

The world is your oyster when it comes to designing with water, and you can get very creative, so it really is a great way to imprint your own personality in the space. Creating a custom water feature that suits your style, as I have (see pp.104–107), brings a charming personal touch to the space.

How long it takes 1 weekend **Best time to do** spring, summer, or fall

Project
How to build a sunken water feature

This project is based on my DIY water feature that uses a repurposed antique water carrier on a bed of cobbles. The water carrier belonged to my late grandfather—he was quite the collector—and I must admit, it's the star of the show!

Before you start

All you need are a few materials, a good pump, and some digging power, and you can create something that has meaning and is personal to you.

You'll need a sump, which is a large, lined cavity in the ground for holding water, similar to a pond. The size of your sump depends on your design. It should be able to hold the water that drains from the feature while the pump is off, plus a little more to allow for evaporation and splashing. For smaller features, a sump that holds 6½–10 gallons (30–45 liters) should be sufficient. For larger features, 22 gallons (100 liters) or more may be necessary.

In my project, the sump is about 36 in (900 mm) in diameter and 36 in (900 mm) deep, which is quite extensive, and you could halve the depth. It will just need some extra topping up during the summer as small sumps evaporate more quickly than big ones.

You can also buy prefabricated sumps in different sizes. You just dig the hole and place the sump inside without the need for pond liner.

MATERIALS
- Building sand
- Butyl rubber pond liner
- Pond pump
- Hose for pump
- Jubilee clips
- Conduit for cables
- Galvanized grid
- Water feature of choice
- Marine sealant
- Cobbles
- Plants

TOOLS
- Tape measure
- Spray paint
- Post hole digger or spade
- Iron bar
- Hose

Opposite In addition to the soothing sound of running water, my water feature is one of the key focal points in the garden.

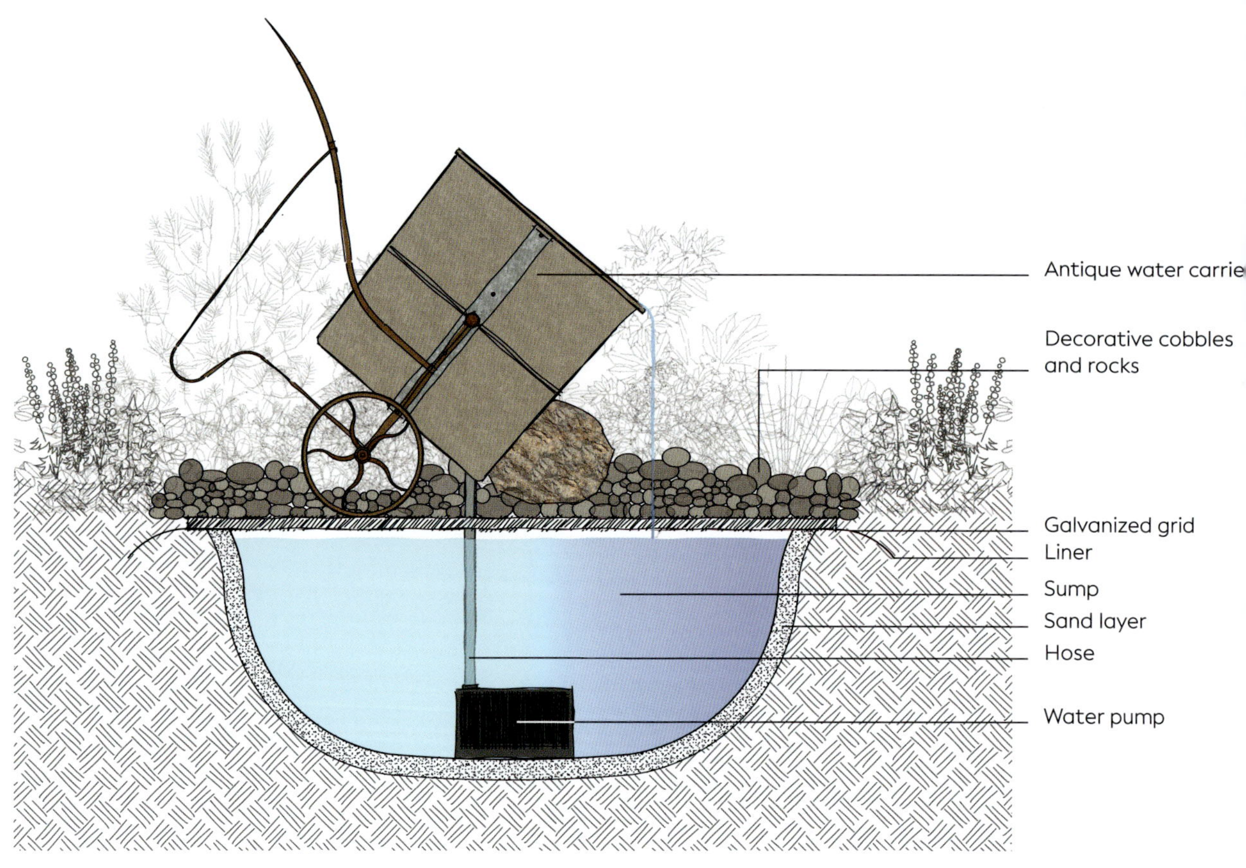

01

Dig the sump hole

Start by clearing the area where the water feature will go, removing any sharp rocks, grass, and plants. Mark out the sump diameter with spray paint and then start digging. Depending on the ground, this may be quite physical, especially if you're working with clay, chalk, or compacted soil. My trusty iron bar and post hole digger worked wonders for this stage of the project.

02

Prepare the sump

Once your sump hole is at the right diameter and depth, remove any sharp objects such as stones from the base and walls to prevent liner tears. Add a 2-in (50-mm) layer of building sand to the bottom and sides, if not too vertical, to provide a cushioned, even base.

03

Line the sump

Install a butyl rubber pond liner, ensuring it's large enough to cover the hole with at least a 3-ft (1-m) overlap at the top. The liner will be held in place by the weight of the water, and this excess helps to anchor it. Liners can be unwieldy, so an extra pair of hands can be helpful here. Gently press the liner into the hole, aiming to remove as many creases as possible.

04

Insert the pump and fill

Attach a long hose to the pump's output using a jubilee clip. This will carry water up to the above-ground feature. Place your pump at the bottom of the sump on flat ground.

If the power cord won't reach a nearby power source, you may need a qualified electrician to extend it. Protect any exposed cables with conduit, especially if you later intend to bury them.

Once the pump is in place, use a hose to fill the sump with water.

05

Put the grid in place

Add a galvanized grid cover over the sump, slightly wider than the hole. You can buy these grids from an aquatic retailer or online, or you can make something similar yourself. The grid should have a small access hole to reach the pump for routine maintenance. Thread the hose through the grid, positioning it above water level.

07

Add cobbles and planting

Test the set-up by turning on the power to ensure it's working as planned, adjusting the pump flow if needed. Once you're satisfied, cover the area with decorative cobbles and rocks for a rustic look. Make sure they're large enough so they don't fall through the grid. Add some gravel-friendly planting around the feature for a natural, pollinator-attracting finish.

06

Install the water feature

Install the above-ground feature. I drilled a hole into the tank of the water carrier before feeding the hose through, sealing it in place with marine sealant. For a cascading effect, I tilted the carrier and secured it with rocks.

CREATING A POND

Creating a pond is a similar process, except that the pump is housed underground adjacent to the pond rather than in a sump. The pump will stop the water from getting stagnant, prevent algae buildup, and improve oxygenation, which is important if you plan to have fish. Planting contributes to the pond ecosystem, helping to filter the water and creating habitats for beneficial insects, frogs, and other wildlife. Be sure to also provide a beach area for wildlife to access the pond easily.

Plant supports

At some point during your gardening journey, you will no doubt need to introduce plant supports for growing some of your favorite plants. There's an abundance of different supports available, from homemade pyramids to grand obelisks, so it's important to understand how they work, what function they serve, and which supports are most appropriate for your beloved plants.

Much like outdoor structures, plant supports can play a vital role in adding a framework, height, and year-round interest to a space. So think about plant supports as another way to elevate your design and overall landscaping appeal.

Obelisks

Obelisks stand tall and narrow in a border and are generally made from metal. They are great for climbing roses, sweet peas, and clematis. A succession of obelisks through a large, herbaceous border, for example, can bring interest as everything else around them goes dormant over winter.

Arches

Use arches for framing walkways and seating areas. They are generally made from metal or wood and are suitable for more heavy-duty climbers, such as climbing and rambling roses, honeysuckle, and jasmine.

Opposite 'Malvern Hills', one of my favorite rambling roses, covers this Roman arch framing the entrance to my garden.

Hooped supports

Hooped supports are perfect for shrubs and tall, flopping perennials. They are generally made from metal and are great for plants such as shrub roses, hydrangeas, and salvias.

Wired supports

Sometimes, a simple wire system affixed to a wall or fence using galvanized steel wires and vine eyes is all you need. These are excellent for training heavy climbers like rambling roses or espaliered fruit trees.

Trellises and lattices

Trellises help to maximize vertical growing space with climbing plants. They're easily attached to fences, walls, or other structures, and are available in a range of sizes, styles, and materials. Lattices can be used to support tall perennials or favorite ornamentals, as well as creating visual interest. On the following pages, I'll show you how to create a grid-style rustic planting lattice made from coppiced hazel.

How long it takes 3–4 hours **Best time to do** late winter or spring

Project
How to build a hazel lattice

This hazel lattice can be used in many different settings, from growing cut flowers to favorite ornamentals. It's very straightforward to build and with minimal cost.

Sourcing materials

If you have hazel growing in your yard, you can use hazel poles for plant supports. If not, you can use bamboo as a substitute. Bamboo is widely available from large garden centers or by mail order.

I tend to use much thicker pieces of hazel for the uprights because some of the timber is directly in the ground, and thicker pieces will decompose more slowly. You can use treated timber or chestnut poles for added longevity of your corner posts.

Set the height of your supports

It's important to set the heights of your outer frame to accommodate the growing height of plants you intend to grow through the lattice. For example, I want to grow delphiniums through this structure. They are tall perennials, so I want to ensure they have adequate support. I've created two layers, one at 18 in (450 mm) above the ground and the other at around 36 in (900 mm). Having two levels with even intervals between them will ensure the plants are well supported at the top and bottom.

You may have already sown seeds or put your plants in the ground before you started building your support. If not, planting after you've finished building the support, placing potted plants exactly where the squares are positioned, is a good way to ensure your plants grow perfectly through the structure.

Mark the heights you need on your corner posts so you know where the hazel poles will go.

MATERIALS

Hazel poles of different thicknesses

Timber screws: 3 in (75 mm) (suitable for the thickness of your wood)

Twine

TOOLS

Hand saw

String line and iron pins

Spade or post hole digger

Builder's square

Drill or screwdriver

Tip

Pre-drill the screw holes for your hazel poles for each step to avoid any wood splitting.

LATTICE IN A BORDER

If you are going to install the lattice on a patch of bare ground or in your border, determine the overall length and width of your support framework. Mark out a perfectly square area and position your uprights in the corners of your marked-out zone. Push them in as far as they can possibly go—they should feel firm. If you're on solid ground, you may want to dig them in and backfill. Use a level to make sure they are going in straight.

01

Fix the corner uprights

You can push the uprights directly into the ground, or you can secure them to the inside corners of a raised bed using timber screws, as I am here. I don't need to determine the length and width of my grid system because I'm using the dimensions of my raised bed. If your posts are too tall, you can cut them down to size at the end of the build.

02

Create the outer frame

Once the corners are in, it's time to create the outer frame. Cut your sides slightly longer than you need for the length and width of your space—you can cut them to size once they are in place. Secure the sides at your chosen heights with timber screws. Since hazel is a natural timber and won't be completely straight, you will have to judge this by eye.

Secure all of your sides, and if you are creating multiple layers, repeat the same process for all layers. Then trim the ends.

03

Add the runners

Once your sides are in, you need to add your runners lengthwise through the middle of the framework to create a grid-like lattice structure. I want my squares to be roughly 24 x 24 in (600 x 600 mm). Space your runners according to the types of plants you plan to grow through the structure. Affix the runners to the sides with timber screws.

04

Create the lattice

For the lattice, I used slightly thinner, pliable pieces of hazel because I want to weave the hazel widthwise from each side through the runners to the other side.

If you have more than two central runners, they stay in place very nicely. Sometimes two runners can move around, so you may decide to secure them in with smaller timber screws.

Cut your hazel slightly larger than you need so the ends overlap. Slide them in at the spacing you have decided for your lattice and secure to the outer frame with twine. You're aiming to create even squares.

05

Trim and plant it up

Walk around the structure and trim off any excess hazel for a neater finish. Then add your plants.

Tip

Every year, check for any rotten, loose, or broken hazel poles and replace them when required.

Opposite There we have it—a rustic, hazel lattice for growing vegetables, cut flowers, or beautiful ornamentals and a statement piece for any space.

Compost

Soil health is the absolute key to achieving a thriving, biodiverse garden full of life, and compost is an essential ingredient to boost the health of your garden's soil. We use compost for mulching our beds and borders, planting, seed sowing, and all-around garden maintenance.

Why make compost?

Not only does compost provide organic matter for plants to grow, it can also improve the structure and aeration of overworked soil. Add fresh, organic compost to your beds and borders, and watch the garden reward you all season long.

Making your own compost is one way of contributing to a more sustainable way of living. Recycling food scraps and plant material reduces the amount of waste being sent to landfills and decreases the carbon footprint of transportation. Creating your own compost also means you can recycle and reuse most of the organic matter your garden and household generates, giving vital nutrients back to the garden to improve soil health and promote biodiversity.

I've found that creating my own compost has also saved me time and money—time in lugging bags of compost up and down the yard and getting rid of green waste, and money from not needing to buy any compost from local garden centers—it's a no-brainer!

Homemade compost varies in appearance, depending on what goes into it. Your compost is ready when it's reduced to around half the volume and has a good dark-brown color. Don't worry if there are still some lumps in it!

COMPOSTING MATERIALS

ONE-THIRD BROWN | **TWO-THIRDS GREEN**

Carbon-rich materials, which are referred to as brown materials, include organic matter such as:

- **twigs and woody plant trimmings**
- **cardboard and paper**
- **straw and hay**
- **dry leaves**
- **sawdust**

Nitrogen-rich materials, which are referred to as green materials, consist of organic matter such as:

- **fresh plant trimmings**
- **lawn clippings**
- **food scraps, such as vegetable peels**
- **weeds**
- **coffee grounds**
- **tea leaves**
- **hair and animal fur**

How do we make compost?

Simply put, compost is organic matter derived from breaking down carbon and nitrogen-rich materials. There is some basic science to understand in order to create your own compost. For organic matter to break down, it's important to have the right balance of green and brown materials combined with oxygen, and this trio will ignite the decomposition process.

Ratios are also important. I prefer to use a ratio of two-thirds green materials to one-third brown materials, but other gardeners use a ratio such as 25:75 or 50:50. That's the beauty of making your own compost—you get to perfect the blend.

Remember that too much of one material can impact the speed of decomposition. If you have a compost heap full of green materials and little to no brown materials, for example, it will become a wet, soggy mess and start to smell. In this case, the compost heap lacks oxygen—it's anaerobic. Since oxygen is a key component to the decomposition process, it's important to bring in more brown materials for structure and to create air pockets so oxygen can circulate. On the flip side, if your compost heap is predominantly brown materials, it will be very dry and lacking any moisture to aid decomposition, so balance is essential.

In addition to getting the right balance of materials, I also recommend you vary the materials going into your heap, because too much of one can create a compost that's very high in a single micronutrient as opposed to a well-balanced blend. By mixing up your ingredients, you will create a nutrient-diverse compost that's perfect for the garden.

There are multiple ways to make compost, from hot bins to worm bins, but one of the simplest ways to make compost is by cold composting. The good news is that you can create your very own cold composter for the price of some screws and a few hours' work on the weekend, and in this section, I'll show you how.

How long it takes 3–4 hours **Best time to do** anytime of year

Project

How to build a compost bay

This is a very simple project to build your own compost bay using some old wooden pallets, a few screws, and, of course, some material to compost.

Source your pallets

You will need to source some wooden pallets. People often leave pallets outside their houses, and they might well be grateful if you ask to take them off their hands. There is often an abundance of pallets at local builders' depots and stores, and most of the time, people are happy for you to have them. Just check you can take them beforehand.

Set out the site

Ideally, you want to site your compost bay on a flat, leveled area which will make things significantly easier when putting it together. You do not need to create a concrete or hard base for it to rest on—compost heaps should be sited directly on the ground to allow beneficial microorganisms and earthworms to get in and out of the compost heap easily.

Don't site your bay next to the house, because compost bays can sometimes smell, and if you are adding food scraps, they can potentially attract rodents. It's best to site your bay at the back of your yard and out of sight, if you have the space.

MATERIALS

3 pallets of the same size

Sleeper screws: 6 x 1/4in (150 x 6.7mm) (adjust according to the size of your pallets)

Plywood or extra pallet for front (optional)

Mesh (optional)

Brown and green material for composting

TOOLS

Spade or rake

Blocks for balancing (optional)

Drill or screwdriver

01

Position the sides

Once you've leveled the space with a spade or rake, put the back of the bay in position. Use some blocks (or an extra pair of hands) to keep it in place. Then place the side pallets flush against the back pallet.

02

Secure the pallets

Secure the side pallets to the back using sleeper screws. Most pallets have a thicker block at each end that's perfect for screwing through because it allows a stronger hold. Use one screw each at the top, middle, and bottom of the pallets.

03

Secure the front

Adding a front to the bay will keep your compost heap contained. Simply affix another pallet or piece of plywood in the same way. Here I used a piece of removable plywood for the front. If the bay is on a slightly uneven base, you can use wooden blocks to prop up the front to the right level. If you like, add hooks or rails to slot the front on so you can easily drop it in and pull it out.

04

Fill the bay

Now for the fun part. You can line the bay with mesh to stop compost from spilling out. Remember your ratios (see p.115). It's a good idea to add a layer of woody or twiggy organic matter at the bottom, such as yew hedge trimmings, which will allow oxygen to get in at the bottom of the pile and rise through the heap.

Think of your compost heap as a lasagna: work in thin layers and try to spread your material evenly across the surface, which will stop the heap from getting saturated and improve the rate of decomposition.

Tip

You can cover your filled heap with a tarp to stop excess moisture from getting in during the winter months. In the summer, this isn't always necessary.

Plant

Once you've built the bare bones of the space, it's time for planting. Plants are what bring your garden to life and set the mood. I think of this part of the project like garnishing a delicious plate of food, something I take from my cheffing days.

In this chapter, we'll look at planting design principles, planting styles, and what plants to choose, as well as some of my favorite plants and those suited to challenging areas. There are step-by-step instructions on planting a hedge, tree, bare-root roses, perennials, and bulbs, and how to lay turf. We'll also look at some propagation techniques you can use throughout the year to create lots of new plants for free.

Planting design principles

Here, we'll cover some of the basics of planting design so you can pull together your very own curated planting plan for your new garden. It can also be helpful when thinking about planting design to reflect on the gardens you like and why. Think about gardens you've visited—what were you drawn to and why, and what type of planting did they have? The five main areas to consider are structure, form, movement, rhythm, and color.

Start with structure

Structure is where you should start when compiling your plant list. Think of it as the skeleton of your garden: how will your garden look when everything dies back over winter?

Trees and shrubs are your core structural plants when it comes to planning your planting scheme. Start with the core structural plants and then infill with grasses, herbaceous perennials (plants with nonwoody stems that live for more than two years), and ground-cover plants. Having a good backbone of trees, shrubs, and perennials is the key to a winning planting scheme and ensuring seasonal interest.

Follow with form

Form is what I have front and center of my mind when making any changes in the garden or adding new plants to the borders. Form is often displayed by the overall shape and texture of a plant through its life cycle, such as the leaf and flower shapes and seed heads. Typically, form is based on the shapes of the flower heads, and the different categories include: umbels, such as angelica and yarrow; racemes, such as delphiniums and wisteria; spires, such as foxgloves; plumes, such as astilbes; daisies, such as rudbeckias; buttons, such as *Phlomis*; and balls, such as alliums.

Opposite This bed has plants that all offer different features of interest. *Amelanchier lamarckii* brings height, structure, and seasonal color, and I've underplanted it with evergreen shrubs, perennials, grasses, and bulbs for year-round interest.

Movement in plants

Movement has a huge impact on how we experience a garden. It provides visual interest and stimulates the senses as we journey through a space. Tall grasses and perennials swaying in a naturalistic garden create a lovely, flowing look to a border and provide a calming feeling. Movement can also be achieved with trees: as they move in the wind, the sound of the leaves creates a soothing backdrop. Formal gardens with structural shrubs, such as clipped topiary, will feel more structured and static.

I've planted *Echinops ritro* and *Verbena bonariensis* throughout the mid-layer of this border. The flowering form repeats through the space, creating a cohesive look and feel to the planting.

Creating rhythm

Rhythm (and I don't mean in the dancing sense) draws the eye through the garden, creating a sense of flow and movement. Good rhythm can unite a garden with its surroundings and connect spaces, such as a flowerbed in the foreground chiming with another at the back. Plants should work in harmony with their surrounding features, helping to link a space with the landscape beyond.

Rhythm works well in several ways: repeating the same plant in groups, echoing flower forms or leaf shapes, or unifying with a consistent flowering color. Repeat planting also helps restrict the species of plants used, creating strong, bold effects as opposed to a scattered look and feel.

You can use repetition in flowering formations and foliage to create a cohesive and harmonious look in a border. For example, plants like perovskias and *Veronicastrum* both produce flowering spires. Repeating these spires throughout a design creates a stunning visual impact.

Similarly, repetition in your color palette can unite a space beautifully. Using different plants within the same color group is an excellent way to tie the design together. For example, *Geranium* 'Rozanne' has a stunning purple hue that works beautifully at the front of the border, especially when repeated in groups in a long stretch of planting. Adding another purple or lilac flowering species to the mid-layer of a border, like perovskia 'Blue Spire', helps to unify the planting, creating a connection between different species through the colors they share.

Creating rhythm can be instantaneous, but realistically, it takes a number of years to get it down to a fine art. You can lift and move plants in spring or fall to create desired effects, and self-seeding will naturally help to build rhythm in a border, but it's always good practice to think about rhythm from the outset. That way, you give yourself the best possible chance of creating a lovely space with cohesion throughout.

USE ODD NUMBERS

Using odd numbers is a design principle that's followed in both interior and garden design. It forces the eye to explore and creates dynamic and rhythmic visual interest. Planting in even numbers is more static and less stimulating visually.

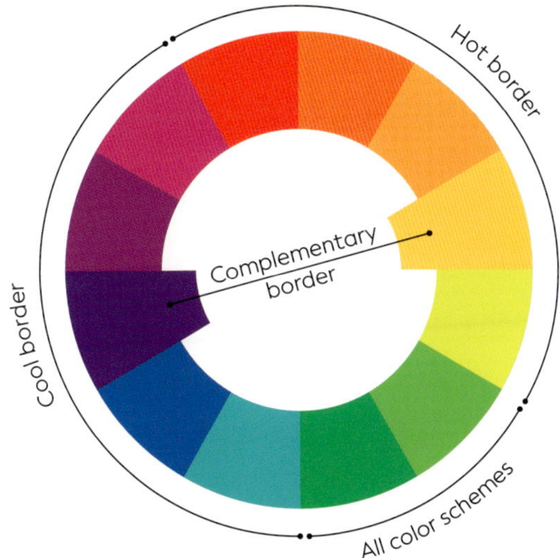

The color wheel
The color wheel can help to identify complementary (opposite) colors and those that can be used in hot and cool borders.

Injecting color

For me, color is the least impactful of these five principles. Color comes and goes throughout the seasons, which is why it's important to focus on structure, form, movement, and rhythm first. Color clearly plays a critical role in setting the mood of a space, but it shouldn't define it, unless, of course, you've purposely curated a classic white garden or hot border where color is central to the theme.

The color wheel (see left) is a fantastic tool to use, helping you identify complementary colors, which contrast and are opposite each other on the wheel, and adjacent colors, which blend in tone and are next to each other. Slight variations in colors blend well together, creating a tone for planting—for example, the cool colors of blue and purple, or the hot colors of red and orange.

You can use the color wheel to create an effective color palette. I'm naturally drawn to complementary colors, which stand out, and oranges and purples shine bright in my garden.

Color all comes down to personal preference and there are no strict rules. Gardens should reflect the gardener's personality, so if you would like to go for the pick-and-mix approach, go for it—there's no judgment here!

Aster × *frikartii* 'Mönch' is one of my favorite late-summer perennials: the purple hue of the petals contrasts beautifully with the yellow center.

Planting for impact

Now we're going to explore different methods to create impact with your planting. There are no strict rules for planting a garden, and everyone has their own tastes and preferences. However, there are some best practices and techniques that can truly unlock your garden's potential and deliver that wow factor.

A single tree underplanted with ornamental grasses in a large pot will create a real statement in any garden setting.

Bigger is better

Be bold with your planting, whether with plants, borders, or pots. You may think that if you have a small space, you can't plant a large tree, but actually, planting big, bold plants in small places often creates the illusion of a bigger space. Similarly with pots: one massive statement pot with an attractive tree and underplanting has far more impact than lots of small pots scattered around.

Grouping plants

When you put plants in groups, think about scale and proportion to create the right balance for planting. For example, planting a single helenium or rudbeckia next to a medium-size shrub is going to look out of proportion, whereas if you plant multiple heleniums or rudbeckias next to that same shrub, the ratios appear more balanced. Remember that planting in odd numbers creates visual interest (see p.122).

Layer your planting

Natural environments, such as forests and woodlands, have several layers, including a tree layer, shrub layer, herbaceous perennials, and ground cover. An impactful planting plan often replicates the different layers found in nature, so if space allows, create beds or borders deep enough to accommodate more than one plant's ultimate spread. That way, plants can be placed in front of or behind each other, which will provide depth and layering to your planting.

Create seasonal interest

Plants change and mature with the seasons, so when you combine them well, you can create some amazing displays throughout the year. The key to a strong garden is to maximize interest throughout the seasons with your planting, and this is often more challenging than people think.

Spring and summer are jam-packed with ideas and inspiration. They are the easiest seasons to get your planting right thanks to the sheer number of options available. You can combine flower forms and choose from an array of different colors.

Fall and winter are a little trickier, because the plant palette is slightly more restricted. This is where evergreen plants come into their own, or plants that have more than one feature of interest. For example, Tibetan cherry (*Prunus serrula*) has lovely yellow and orange fall foliage, as well as striking bark that can be admired when the leaves drop.

You can use filler plants, bulbs, or annuals to extend the seasons, so try to think about your garden through the seasons to ensure it has color in fall and winter.

MOVING PLANTS

To create an impactful planting plan, you might want to move plants that are in the wrong place or have outgrown their spot. Maybe you have a beloved shrub at the front of a border that would look better farther back.

Spring and fall are the best times to do it. Dig generously around the root ball. You want to get as much of the soil and root system intact as you can, with minimal disturbance, to give the plant the best possible chance of survival in its new site.

Then dig a hole to the depth of the root ball and two to three times the diameter. Add the plant, backfill with a mixture of soil and fresh compost, firm it in, and give the plant a good soak. Keep it regularly watered so it can settle into its new home.

Planting styles

Having a specific planting style in mind will inform the type of planting you want to incorporate into your garden, and the principles of planting design (see pp.120–125) can be applied to any type of planting style. A garden theme or planting style does not necessarily lead to good design, but good design can influence how strong your planting style or theme turns out. You may decide you have a particular style in mind or are looking to explore options. Here we look at some common planting styles.

Cottage garden

A cottage garden is typically an informal planting plan consisting of a broad range of trees, shrubs, herbaceous perennials, climbers, and annuals. There may be a mass of color with edible plants growing in the borders. When I think of cottage-garden planting, I think of delphiniums, foxgloves, and hollyhocks with rustic sweet pea supports popping up throughout a border—there's something very charming and magical about this look.

Formal garden

The formal garden style dates back centuries and is traditionally known for its symmetrical, geometric look formed by neatly clipped hedging and topiary. Structure is fundamental to the design, and it's a style that will look clean and sharp throughout the seasons—perfect for the perfectionist gardener.

Gravel garden

Gravel gardens are an increasingly popular style due to their low maintenance and sustainability benefits of minimizing water consumption. They are generally made by mulching what is predominantly poor-quality, free-draining soil with a fine stone aggregate (½in/10mm or less) to a minimum depth of 6in (150mm).

Plant selection and weed-suppressing gravel keep this style low maintenance. Typically, drought-tolerant plants do not need much, or even any, water by design. These might include grasses, perovskias, euphorbias, and alpines. Self-seeding plants are generally encouraged to create a free-flowing and natural look for a gravel garden.

My style of planting is naturalistic, using ornamental grasses and perennials with a slight nod to what you would expect to find in a natural prairie.

Jungle or tropical garden

If you would like to achieve a luxuriant look, the jungle garden may be the option for you. It can be achieved using commonly grown hardy plants, such as *Fatsia japonica*, lupins, and heucheras—it's about big, bold leaf forms and plenty of green. The style is becoming increasingly popular in urban settings, carpeting small spaces with a mass of jungle-like foliage to create what feels like an enchanting rainforest. Urban settings are particularly suited to this style because of the warmer microclimates found there, allowing less hardy and nonnative varieties to grow where there is shelter from prevailing winds and warm, sunny walls.

Naturalistic garden

Out of all of the styles, the naturalistic garden speaks to my personal preferences the most. This style is oriented toward using plants that thrive in the local area. They look in keeping with the environment beyond, such as a woodland-style garden next to a natural woodland.

What's your style?

These are some of the more commonly known planting styles, but there is an abundance of different planting styles out there today, such as the Japanese garden, and they keep evolving.

Think about what style you are more drawn to and why. Does a particular style make you feel a certain way? It may bring back childhood memories, for instance, or it may simply be the look you'd love to achieve. I find it useful to go to local flower shows for inspiration, which is something you may consider if you're not sure what you're drawn to.

Choosing your plants

I like to think of planting from an artistic perspective—we are all artists creating beautiful paintings in the garden using color and form as our painter's palette. This is where you can really express yourself and the special thing about gardening is that it's constantly evolving. Plants change with the seasons as well as from year to year, with annuals coming and going and perennials growing and spreading—and you can always move plants around too (see p.125).

Consider the function

Plants are versatile and can be used in a multitude of ways, depending on your wants and needs. I like to think about a plant's function at the beginning rather than the end of the planting design process. Plants can:

- create structure
- provide visual interest
- form screening for privacy and create distinct zones
- provide scent and other sensory qualities
- create seasonal displays
- form focal points.

An important factor in your plant choice should be what you want from your garden, so refer back to your overall vision (see p.11). Do you want your space to have different zones, such as dining and play areas? If so, you might want plants to delineate those areas. Do you need to use plants for privacy or screening? Are you planning to sit outside in the evening? If so, you might consider night-scented plants. Do you want to maximize seasonal or sensory interest? Identify the role and function your plants will play and make plant choices accordingly.

Right plant, right place

It's important to select plants that will work with your plan and your conditions. The principle of right plant, right place will save you so much time and money further down the line (see also pp.134–137). Don't fall into the trap of just buying what looks great in the garden center (we've all made that mistake). Do your research and think not only about seasonality and function, but also what is suited to your space.

The range of plants available is substantial—thousands and thousands of different species—so it can be overwhelming at first. Start by breaking it down into the core categories of trees, shrubs, climbers, herbaceous perennials, grasses, annuals, and bulbs. Take a look around your neighborhood to see what's thriving in similar conditions, what you like the look of and why, and whether it could be included in your plan.

There are many apps that can help you identify a plant just by taking a photo of it, which is particularly helpful if you have no plant knowledge (see p.186). Start to build a wish list of plants that are suited to your outdoor conditions.

Seasonal maintenance

All plants require a level of maintenance, so it's important to review your overall goal and vision for the space. Define a planting plan that aligns with how much time you can commit to maintaining the garden in the long run (see pp.28–33). I have spacious herbaceous borders full of perennials and shrubs, and they keep me extremely busy. If you're looking for low maintenance, your choice of plants will be guided by this.

Opposite Color extends from late summer well into fall in this border of drought-tolerant perennials, shrubs, and grasses, which thrive in the dry conditions.

Height and spread

Once you've decided which plants you'd like to have, make sure you look at the eventual height and spread of the plants—this information is generally found on the back of plant labels or you can look it up online. Gardeners often make the mistake of overspending and bringing in too many plants, and then have to thin out the beds and borders the following year. It's better to have some space so the plants can grow into it rather than a packed border with everything squashed from day one.

My favorite plants

I have tried and experimented with many different plants over the years and have started to build a repertoire of plants that I know do very well in my garden and beyond. A lot of the plants that I grow are extremely hardy and drought tolerant, and they need to be, given that I have a sloping yard with chalky soil. For some inspiration, here are some of my all-time favorite plants that I currently grow.

Trees

- *Amelanchier lamarckii*
- *Cornus kousa*
- *Magnolia grandiflora*
- *Prunus serrula*
- *Prunus × subhirtella* 'Autumnalis'
- *Sorbus* 'Autumn Spire'

Shrubs

- *Buddleia* 'Miss Ruby'
- *Ceratostigma willmottianum*
- *Euonymus alatus*
- *Pittosporum tenuifolium* 'Golf Ball'
- *Rosa* 'The Lark Ascending'
- *Salvia* 'Blue Spire'
- *Salvia* 'Pink Pong'

Herbaceous perennials

- *Aster × frikartii* 'Mönch'
- *Eutrochium maculatum* Atropurpureum Group
- *Helenium* 'Moerheim Beauty'
- *Penstemon digitalis* 'Husker Red'
- *Rudbeckia fulgida* var. *sullivantii* 'Goldsturm'
- *Salvia nemorosa* 'Caradonna'
- *Veronicastrum virginicum* 'Fascination'

Grasses

- *Calamagrostis × acutiflora* 'Karl Foerster'
- *Miscanthus sinensis* 'Morning Light'
- *Miscanthus sinensis* 'Strictus'
- *Sesleria fallalis*
- *Stipa gigantea*
- *Stipa tenuissima*

Climbers and ramblers

- *Hydrangea petiolaris*
- *Rosa* 'Ghislaine de Féligonde'
- *Rosa* 'Malvern Hills'
- *Rosa* 'Paul's Himalayan Musk'
- *Trachelospermum jasminoides*

Bulbs, corms, and rhizomes

- *Allium sphaerocephalon*
- *Crocosmia × crocosmiiflora* 'George Davison'
- *Crocosmia* 'Lucifer'
- *Iris germanica*

Opposite, clockwise from top left *Rosa* 'The Lark Ascending', *Aster × frikartii* 'Mönch', *Iris germanica*, and *Miscanthus sinensis* 'Strictus'.

Right plant, right place

There are bound to be areas in your yard where plants seem to struggle. Exposed or shady spots may be the culprit, or perhaps it's down to heavy clay or acidic soil. There are plants that can thrive in these conditions, and it's just a question of choosing the right plants for the right place.

Shady areas

Most yards will inevitably have a shady area—less than three hours in full sun—whether that be under a tree, a north-facing border, or a small corner next to the house. With a vast selection of shade-tolerant plants available, these spots can be transformed into lush, unique garden sanctuaries. Plants that do well in shady areas include early flowering bulbs, ferns, and mosses.

Shade lovers

Dryopteris filix-mas
Epimedium grandiflorum
Helleborus orientalis
Heuchera 'Plum Pudding'
Pulmonaria longifolia

Sunny sites

This is where a plant's origin comes into play—if plants are native to hot and dry climates, they will be well suited to these types of conditions. A south-facing, sheltered space can feel sweltering in the summer, so you will need plants that love the sun and are adapted to growing in these conditions.

Typically, plants with fine hairs on the leaf surface or waxy leaves are good at deflecting the sun's rays. Scented plants have a unique way of protecting themselves against the sun—they produce an array of aromatic oils that act as a defensive layer. Succulents are perhaps the best-known plant group to be well adapted to heat—they store water in their leaves to prevent dehydration and can go for weeks without needing water.

Sun seekers

Euphorbia characias subsp. *wulfenii*
Helenium 'Moerheim Beauty'
Rudbeckia fulgida var. *sullivantii* 'Goldsturm'
Salvia 'Blue Spire'
Stachys byzantina

Left, from top *Helleborus orientalis*, *Heuchera* 'Plum Pudding', *Euphorbia characias* subsp. *wulfenii*, and *Rudbeckia fulgida* var. *sullivantii* 'Goldsturm'.

Exposed areas

Spaces exposed to high winds create some of the most trying conditions for plants, and coastal gardens like mine fall into this category. Wind is a silent killer for plants because it dries their roots out and often leads to wind rock, loosening the soil and disturbing the roots. In these conditions, it's important to choose plants that are tough, drought tolerant, and adapted for the conditions, otherwise they are destined to fail.

Plants that allow wind to travel through them are better suited to exposed sites, because it puts less pressure on the roots. Grasses take particularly well to exposed conditions because the wind can travel easily through their core structure.

Wind-resistant plants
Calamagrostis × *acutiflora* 'Karl Foerster'
Ceratostigma plumbaginoides
Elaeagnus × *submacrophylla*
Hippophae rhamnoides
Salvia rosmarinus
Stipa gigantea
Verbena bonariensis

Heavy clay

Soil that is made up of heavy clay is often one of the most difficult environments to garden in. In the summer heat, clay hardens and dries up; in winter when it rains, the clay gets saturated and extremely sticky. In both scenarios, the growing conditions are tough for plants to thrive.

However, clay soils are very rich and fertile with a great foundational structure, and they can be a fantastic growing medium for a broad range of plants if soil conditioners and organic matter are added to improve airflow and add vital nutrients. Plants such as some geranium and hydrangea species can thrive in clay.

Suited to clay
Alchemilla mollis
Geranium 'Patricia'
Hydrangea species
Osmanthus × *burkwoodii*
Viburnum × *bodnantense* 'Dawn'

Left, from top *Verbena bonariensis, Stipa gigantea, Alchemilla mollis,* and *Hydrangea* 'Preziosa'.

Acidic soil

It's important to understand the soil pH requirements of your plants before planting them (see p.12). You will have either acidic, neutral, or alkaline soil to work with, but moderation is the key to getting the most out of your growing conditions. If your soil is too acidic, it can cause unfavorable growing conditions for your plants, in which case, adding lime can help regulate the acidity.

There are some benefits to having acidic soil. Slightly acidic soil can increase the availability of certain nutrients to plants, such as iron, manganese, and aluminum, and some plants thrive in acidic soil conditions, such as rhododendrons, camellias, and heathers.

Acid lovers
Anemone × *hybrida* 'Honorine Jobert'
Azalea species
Calluna vulgaris
Camellia species
Rhododendron species

Alkaline soil

Whereas acidic soils have a higher element of key nutrients, such as iron, manganese, and aluminum, alkaline soils (see p.12) have depleted stores of iron, manganese, and zinc, so regular mulching or feeding will be required to improve the nutritional value.

Chalky soils are often high in alkalinity, but there is a broad range of plants that will thrive in these conditions. Some of my favorite prairie-style plants and ornamental grasses thrive in poorer soil conditions, and free-draining, chalky soils lend themselves to the naturalistic style of planting (see p.129).

Since chalky soil is lacking in core nutrients, you will need to improve soil structure and add nutrients by mulching thickly, because some plants need a more humus-rich soil high in nutrient value to thrive.

If you have alkaline soil, you should avoid planting species that prefer acidic soil—instead, consider planting them in containers or in raised beds with plenty of acidic potting mix.

Alkaline lovers
Geranium 'Rozanne'
Miscanthus sinensis 'Morning Light'
Pittosporum tenuifolium
Salvia nemorosa 'Caradonna'
Verbena bonariensis

Left, from top *Anemone* × *hybrida* 'Honorine Jobert', *Rhododendron* 'Hydon Dawn', *Salvia nemorosa* 'Caradonna', and *Geranium* 'Rozanne'.

Opposite My south-facing garden with chalky soil is perfect for my favorite style of naturalistic planting.

How long it takes 2–3 hours **Best time to do** fall

Project
How to plant a hedge

Planting a hedge is one of the most cost-effective ways to create boundaries and add privacy, and you don't need extensive horticultural knowledge to get it done! A hedge not only provides a natural boundary but also creates a vital ecosystem for nesting birds and other wildlife, making your space more biodiverse and eco-friendly.

Planting methods

There are a couple of methods you can use to plant a hedge: either plant each shrub individually, or dig a single, long trench and plant them all at once. I've used the trench method here, which can often save time and ensure an even look across the row.

You can plant hedges from early fall to early spring, when bare-root plants are available. These are sold without soil around the roots and are usually a fraction of the price of potted plants. It's best to plant in fall because the soil is still warm, giving plants time to establish their roots over winter, ready to thrive come spring.

Before you start

You also need to decide on the type of hedge you'd like to plant. If low maintenance is a priority, look for a slower-growing variety such as English yew; if you want color year round, go for evergreen species like Portuguese laurel. Soak the roots in water for at least two hours before planting.

MATERIALS

Mushroom compost or well-rotted manure

Coarse sand (optional)

Compost

Mulch

TOOLS

String line and pins

Spray paint

Spade or mattock

Fork

Cane

HEDGING PLANTS

These are good plants to use for hedging, depending on whether you want a deciduous or evergreen hedge.

Deciduous plants

Beech (*Fagus*)
Hawthorn (*Crataegus*)
Hazel (*Corylus*)
Hornbeam (*Carpinus*)
Japanese rose (*Rosa rugosa*)

Evergreen plants

English yew (*Taxus baccata*)
Griselinia
Holly (*Ilex*)
Leyland cypress, leylandii (x *Cuprocyparis leylandii*)
Portuguese laurel (*Prunus lusitanica*)

01

Clear the site

Start by clearing the area where your hedge will go. Remove any vegetation and obstructions. Stretch a string line along the length of the planned hedge line.

02

Mark the hedge line

Use spray paint to mark the line, using the string line as your guide. This will ensure you dig out your trench in a straight and even line.

03

Dig the trench

Dig a trench that is twice as wide and as deep as the root ball of your hedging plants. Pile the soil on one side of the trench to create a bank; you'll use this soil, mixed with fresh organic matter, to backfill. Aim to keep an even depth along the entire length of the trench.

04

Prepare the trench base

Before placing your plants in the trench, use a fork to loosen up the soil at the base to improve drainage and help roots establish. Add some mushroom compost or well-rotted manure to the bottom of the trench for added nutrients. If your soil is heavy clay, mix in a little coarse sand to enhance drainage.

05

Position the plants

Place your hedging plants in the trench, using the correct spacing for the variety and maturity of your plants. Generally, two to three plants per 3 feet (1 m) creates a dense hedge. For consistent spacing, measure and cut a bamboo cane to the desired spacing length and use it as a guide when positioning the plants.

PLANT A DOUBLE HEDGE

If you want to create a thicker hedge with more instant impact, plant in a slightly wider trench in two rows with equal, offset spacing.

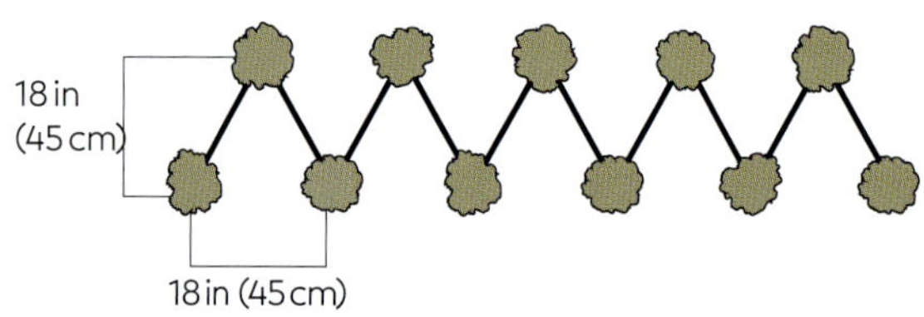

07

Water and mulch

Give the newly planted hedge a generous watering to settle the soil around the roots. Add a layer of mulch, such as bark or wood chips, around the hedge base to help retain moisture and suppress weeds.

06

Backfill and firm up

Once your plants are in place, backfill the trench with the original soil mixed with some fresh compost. Firm the plants in gently but securely, ensuring good soil-to-root contact.

Planting a hedge is a simple, natural way to define spaces and create attractive, eco-friendly borders.

How long it takes 1 hour **Best time to do** fall

Project
How to plant a tree

Every yard should have at least one tree. Trees supply much-needed height, structure, and natural shade to any outdoor space, and used in the right way, they can create a great impact in your space. Trees also provide vital habitats for wildlife.

Before you start

People often believe, mistakenly, that you need a large yard to grow trees, but this is not the case. Small yards lend themselves just as well to trees, and trees can create the optical illusion that the yard is bigger than it actually is. For a yard of any size, it's key to choose a tree that will fit well within the space. Make sure there's enough room for the eventual height and spread, although, of course, you can prune some trees to size.

You can buy trees as potted plants, root balls, or bare-root specimens, each varying in price and requiring a slightly different planting approach. Here, I'm planting a pot-grown tree. If your tree is in a pot, give it a good soak before planting. I like to submerge the pot in water until all the bubbles stop, ensuring it's fully hydrated. If you're planting a root ball, plant it first and water well. See pp.146–147 for how to plant bare-root plants.

You can add mycorrhizal fungi to the planting hole to promote root growth. These beneficial fungi help the plant absorb nutrients and moisture.

It's incredibly satisfying and rewarding planting your very first tree, so let's get to it!

MATERIALS

- Compost
- Fertilizer
- Mycorrhizal fungi (optional)
- Wooden stake
- Rubber tie
- Felting nails
- Well-rotted manure (optional)
- Coarse sand (optional)

TOOLS

- Spade or post hole digger
- Cane
- Fork
- Lump hammer
- Hand saw (optional)

01

Dig the planting hole

Pick your spot then use a spade or post hole digger to dig a square hole deep enough for the root ball and about 1.5 times its diameter. This will allow the roots space to grow with plenty of room to add fresh organic matter to the planting hole.

02

Check the planting hole depth

To confirm the hole is deep enough, place the tree in the hole and put a cane or stick across the hole to check that the base of the stem sits just proud of the soil surface.

03

Plant the tree

Add compost to the base of the hole and fork it in. Place the tree in the hole, ensuring the stem base is just above ground level, and confirm it's vertically straight by stepping back and judging by eye. Loosen the roots before sprinkling a base fertilizer like bonemeal in the hole to aid root development. You can also add mycorrhizal fungi directly to the roots to promote healthy growth.

04

Stake the tree

For single-stem trees, hammer a stake into the ground at a 45-degree angle, facing the prevailing wind. Avoid disturbing the root ball.

05

Secure the tree

Use a rubber tree tie and felting nails to secure the tree to the stake with a figure-eight.

06

Trim the stake

Using a hand saw, trim the stake down if it's too tall.

07

Backfill the hole

Backfill the hole gradually with a mix of the soil you dug out and some fresh compost or well-rotted manure. If your soil drains poorly, mix in some coarse sand. Firm down the soil with your heel as you go.

Tip

If your yard is on a slope, use compost to build a moat to capture the water flowing downhill.

08

Water in

Watering is essential to establish your tree. Give it a thorough soak after planting, and keep watering regularly for the first two years, particularly during spring and summer. This ensures your tree has the best chance of thriving.

HOW TO PLANT A SHRUB

Planting shrubs follows the exact same process as planting a tree except there is no need for staking. Follow the steps outlined here and keep up with routine watering to ensure the success of your shrub.

I planted a mountain ash—*Sorbus* 'Autumn Spire'. It's a lovely tree with a columnar form and has purple, red, and yellow foliage in the fall.

How long it takes 20 minutes **Best time to do** fall or winter

Project
How to plant bare-root roses

Roses are one of my favorite plant groups. Fall is the perfect time to buy them, given it's bare-root season and bare-root roses are a fraction of the price of potted roses. Fall is also the best time to plant roses because it allows them to get settled in over winter.

Before you start

Once your bare-root roses arrive, check them for any damage or disease, and cut off and dispose of any damaged or diseased parts. Soak the plants in water for a minimum of two hours before planting.

Here, I planted a bare-root climbing rose at the base of a dead tree in the middle of the lawn. I wanted to take advantage of the architectural interest of the tree and use it as a natural plant support, with the intention of the rose climbing up through the branches.

MATERIALS

Well-rotted manure

Mycorrhizal fungi (optional)

Compost

TOOLS

Spade or post hole digger

Fork

Cane

01

Prepare the ground

Use a spade or post hole digger to dig a generous-size hole two to three times the width of the root system and about the depth of a spade. Loosen the soil at the bottom of the hole with a fork to help the roots penetrate and anchor in. Using a cane to measure, make sure the crown or knuckle of the rose will be at least 2 in (5 cm) below soil level.

02

Plant your rose

Add a spade of well-rotted manure to the bottom of the hole and add your rose, spreading out the roots evenly. At this stage, you can sprinkle in some mycorrhizal fungi to aid root development.

03

Backfill and water in

Backfill the hole with a mix of soil and fresh compost. Firm the rose in and then give it a good water. Keep on top of watering during the early stages of planting.

Opposite *Rosa* 'Malvern Hills' is a beautiful rambling rose that, unusually for ramblers, repeat flowers.

How long it takes 10+ minutes **Best time to do** fall or spring

Project

How to plant herbaceous perennials

Herbaceous perennials are the volume plants of the garden. For larger borders, I may plant hundreds, but for smaller borders, it's usually in groupings of three or five. I find nothing more exciting than planting perennial beauties as I imagine how they will mature and bring the garden to life.

Before you start

Perennials are straightforward to plant, but it's important to give them the right soil conditions to thrive. I always add extra compost around the planting area, ensuring both the planting hole and surrounding soil have the nutrients the plants need to support their rapid growth.

Start by digging over the ground to loosen the soil, clearing out any weeds, and mixing in fresh compost. This gives the soil a boost and sets the stage for strong growth.

As with trees and shrubs, I soak my perennials in a bucket of water until no more bubbles appear so they're fully hydrated before going into the ground.

MATERIALS

Compost

TOOLS

Spade or post hole digger

01

Set out your plants

Lay out your plants according to their mature height and spread, giving them enough space so they won't need thinning later on. Planting at the recommended distance ensures they'll fill in nicely without overcrowding. Once you've placed everything, step back to get a good look.

02

Dig the planting holes

Use a spade or post hole digger to dig each hole about one and a half times the size of the pot, allowing plenty of room for roots to spread out and establish well.

03

Remove the pot

Carefully remove each plant from its container, teasing out the roots to encourage growth into the surrounding soil.

04

Plant and backfill

Place the plant in its hole, backfill with soil using your hands or a spade, and firm it in. Give the plants a generous drink of water and keep up the routine watering as they settle in, especially during dry spells.

How long it takes 10+ minutes **Best time to do** fall, spring, or summer

Project
How to plant bulbs

There's something incredibly exciting about bulb season. When garden centers fill their shelves with a variety of spring bulbs, it takes me back to childhood trips to the local supermarket, choosing my favorite pick-and-mix. Bulbs are a fantastic way to extend seasonal interest and ensure there's always something to admire in the garden year round.

Planting methods

There are a few methods for planting bulbs depending on where and how you want them to display: scattered in borders, planted into the lawn, or grouped in pots. For planting in lawns, you can lift the turf, as shown opposite, or use a bulb planter.

As a general rule of thumb, plant your bulbs at a depth of two to three times their height. Most bulb packets give clear instructions on planting depth, height, and overall spread, which is always worth a quick glance if you're unsure.

Plant bulbs in pots

Planting bulbs in pots is a great way to create beautiful floral displays throughout the seasons. You can plant up bulbs in pots by layering them, much as you would a lasagna. Plant your largest bulbs first and then gradually layer up your pot with potting mix and smaller bulbs until you reach the top of the container.

TOOLS

Hori hori or trowel (borders)

Spade or bulb planter (lawns)

A bulb lasagna

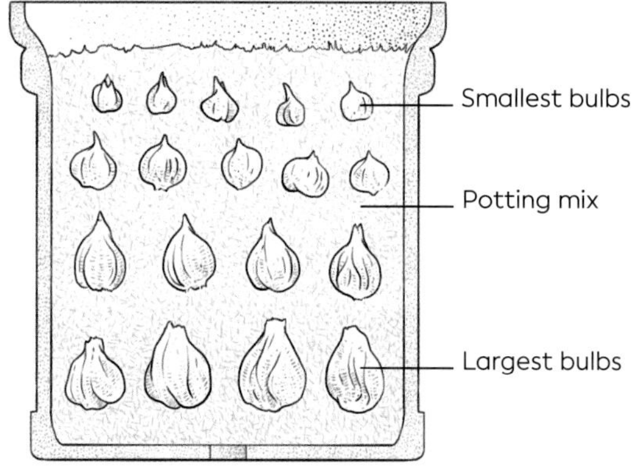

Planting a bulb lasagna is a great way to maximize seasonal interest, with the bulbs flowering at different times.

Border planting

In my own garden, my go-to method is border planting, particularly with spring bulbs such as alliums and daffodils.

01

Scatter the bulbs

For a natural, organic look, scatter the bulbs over the area by throwing them up in the air.

02

Dig the holes

Dig a hole where each bulb falls with a hori hori or trowel to the depth on the packet instructions.

03

Plant the bulbs

With the pointed end facing up, place each bulb in its hole and backfill with soil.

Lawn planting

When planting directly into the lawn, you can take a similar approach.

01

Lift the turf

Plant clusters of bulbs under lifted strips of turf. Use a spade to lift the turf along three sides.

02

Plant the bulbs

With the pointed end facing up, place each bulb on the soil and re-lay the turf on top.

Yellow garlic (*Allium moly*) produces delicate, bright yellow flowers with plenty of star power.

How long it takes 2–3+ hours **Best time to do** fall

Project
How to lay sod

We love lawns, with their neat stripes and carefully maintained appearance. Laying sod is the most straightforward way to go and gives you instant results compared to sowing seed.

Buying turf

You can pick up sod rolls from a garden center or a specialized supplier on the day of laying, or you can order them online for delivery the day before. The rolls come in a standard size, usually 500 sq ft—but each supplier may sell rolls with different dimensions, so it's best to check. The width and length of your lawn will determine how many rolls you'll need per row.

MATERIALS

Topsoil

Sod rolls

TOOLS

Spade or turf cutter

Tiller (optional)

Rake

Scaffolding board or plank

Before you start

You'll need to add new topsoil across the entire space to give your new sod a rich bed in which to establish itself. Determine the amount you need based on your subsoil conditions. If it's poor and mainly clay or rock, bring in a minimum of 4 in (100 mm) good-quality topsoil. If it's fairly decent subsoil, you can work with 2 in (50 mm) of new topsoil.

Ground preparation is key. Start by stripping back any existing vegetation or turf and clearing it away. You can do this with a spade or rent a turf cutter, which I recommend if you're working with a large space.

Top tip

Ideally, lay your sod as soon as possible after buying it to prevent it from drying out. If there's a delay, keep your sod rolls shaded and well watered until you're ready to start.

01

Prepare the ground

Once you've cleared the site, use a tiller or spade to turn over the topsoil, and then rake it over to break up any large clumps, creating a smooth, level surface.

Spread the new topsoil evenly, then tread it down for a firm, even surface, which sets the stage for laying your sod.

02

Lay the sod

Begin by laying a full roll along the edge, pressing it firmly to ensure good contact between the roots and the soil.

Lay the sod in a stretcher-bond pattern (see p.57), staggering each row: after the first full-length roll, start the next with a half roll and so on to avoid lining up the joints. To achieve a seamless look, butt the edges together tightly, "thatching" them together so the roots and grass blades mesh well.

As you work your way across the lawn, use a scaffolding board or plank to kneel on—spreading your weight helps protect the sod and stops the roots from breaking.

03

Tamp down and water

Once all the sod is laid, most areas should already have good soil contact from your weight working across the lawn, but it's worth going over it one final time with the scaffold board or plank to tamp it down, ensuring full contact.

Then give it a thorough soak. Adjust the watering depending on the season: in spring, summer, and fall, watering every other day until it's well established is best.

KEEP OFF THE GRASS!

Don't walk on the grass for a few weeks while it settles—foot traffic can damage new growth and leave indentations. Also try to keep any pets off the lawn as their urine can be very acidic and kill off the top growth.

Plants for free

Who doesn't like a freebie? Propagating plants is one of the best and most cost-effective ways to quickly fill out your beds and borders. Plants can be very expensive when you're starting a new garden from scratch, so learning how to propagate is a great way to save money.

There is a variety of different propagation methods and techniques, and you don't need to be a professional gardener to master the art of propagation—it's all about experimentation and learning through your successes and failures. Here we look at some of the basic propagation techniques, and it's advisable to check the best way to propagate a particular plant.

Layering

Layering might seem very technical, but in fact, it's probably one of the easiest ways to propagate plants. It's best to layer plants in spring or fall, and it's great for plants such as wisteria, *Cornus*, *Salix*, and buddleia.

01

Make an incision

Use clean pruners or a knife to make a 1–2-in (2.5–5-cm) incision in a flexible stem.

02

Pin it down

Pin the stem down in situ using steel pegs and simply let it be. The pinned-down stem will form roots in about 12 months.

03

Sever the stem

Once the layered stem has rooted into the ground, sever it from the parent plant and dig it up. Then either pot it on or plant it out directly into the ground.

Dividing herbaceous perennials

Dividing perennials is a fantastic way to create lots of new plants for free, and it's really straightforward to do. The best time to do it is in fall or spring. Simply dig out a generous amount of the clump and don't be afraid to go at it with your spade—plants like rudbeckia are very forgiving, so don't be shy. Use a spade or back-to-back forks and cut straight through the center of the clump. You can then repeat this process to create quarters, ensuring that there's visible top growth and a good amount of roots intact.

Then replant the divisions. Dig a generous hole, put the plant in, and backfill with some fresh compost mixed with your garden soil, firm it in, and then water it well.

Here I am dividing a clump of rudbeckia that has outgrown its current site.

Basal cuttings

Basal cuttings are taken in early to mid-spring from a tiny slice at the base of the plant—a tuber, rhizome, or part of the crown. Once they've rooted, you can pot them on and harden them off for two weeks to plant out in the summer, or you can keep them under cover until the following spring. Basal cuttings work well with dahlias, lupins, delphiniums, asters, salvias, and phlox, among others, but plants with hollow stems are not suitable.

01

Sever the stem

Select stems around 4–6 in (10–15 cm) tall. Using a clean, sharp knife or pruners, sever the stem at the base of the plant, taking a tiny slice of tuber, rhizome, or crown with it.

02

Trim off foliage

Trim off any excess stems and foliage.

03

Pot up

Pot up your basal cuttings in a potting mix of perlite and peat-free potting mix, and keep them well watered and out of direct sunlight. They usually take about two to four weeks to root.

Take softwood cuttings from green stems, semi-ripe cuttings from stems that have started to turn brown, and hardwood cuttings from mature, brown stems.

Softwood cuttings

You can take softwood cuttings in spring and early summer from many herbaceous perennials, such as hydrangeas, verbenas, *Nepeta*, salvias, lavender, pelargoniums, and penstemons, among others. They are similar to basal cuttings except that you don't need to take a part of the base with your cutting.

01

Cut below a leaf node

Select any nonflowering stems around 4–6 in (10–15 cm) tall. Cut just beneath a leaf node and remove all the lower leaves to reduce transpiration and water loss.

02

Dip in a rooting hormone

To encourage root development, you can score the stem very slightly and dip your cuttings in a rooting hormone. This will encourage root development at both the base of the cutting and farther up the stem.

03

Pot up

Pot the cuttings up and keep them well watered and out of direct sunlight until they have rooted and are ready to pot on.

Semi-ripe cuttings

A semi-ripe cutting is taken from plant material that has started to ripen but is not yet fully mature—hence the name. Simply put, the stems are starting to turn from green to brown.

Semi-ripe cuttings are a great way to propagate shrubs and woody perennials such as lavender, rosemary, hydrangeas, jasmine, and thyme, among others. It's best to take these cuttings in late summer to early fall once new growth has started to ripen.

Follow the exact same procedure as for softwood cuttings. Keep them overwintered under cover and plant out in the spring. Given the maturity of the plant, they are generally more resilient and will tolerate higher levels of plant hormones, which will help them root more easily.

Hardwood cuttings

The method of taking hardwood cuttings differs from that of softwood and semi-ripe cuttings. Generally, you can take hardwood cuttings in the dormant season, just after plants have lost their leaves, or just before spring growth. Most deciduous shrubs take well to propagating through hardwood cuttings.

They take a while to root and will go through a callusing process over winter before roots emerge in spring. The callus is whitish tissue that is essential for root development. You do need to be patient with hardwood cuttings, but they are a fantastic and reliable way to create free plants. They are perfect for creating cheap hedges too.

01

Cut above and below a leaf node

Take cuttings around a pencil thickness and between 6 and 9 in (15 and 23 cm) long. Make your bottom cut just below a leaf node and your top cut just above a leaf node and at an angle. The angle shows where the top of the cutting is and prevents water pooling there.

02

Score the stem

Score the stem at the base very slightly to encourage root development from the base and farther up the stem. Dip the stem in a hormone rooting mix.

03

Pot up or plant out

Plant it directly in the ground, or pot it up and leave it outside. Two-thirds of the stem should be under soil but make sure the angled cut is above the soil. Water well.

Root cuttings

Root cuttings are probably the most challenging of the propagation methods covered here because of the effort in lifting the plant and selecting the right roots to propagate. You can take root cuttings from herbaceous perennials such as anemones, *Echinops*, acanthus, *Verbascum*, and primulas in late fall and winter once the plants are dormant. The method differs depending on whether the plant has thick or thin roots, so double check this.

Thick roots

This method applies to plants with thick roots, such as acanthus and *Verbascum*. Lift the plant and wash the roots before selecting the root to cut. A worthy candidate is a vigorous root of around a pencil thickness. Avoid the wispy, fibrous roots because you will have little success. Cut off a long root at the crown of the plant. Then quickly replant the parent plant and water it so it can settle back in.

Trim off any small, fibrous roots and cut the root into smaller sections of between 2 and 4 in (5 and 10 cm). Cut one end at an angle and the other flat.

Put the root cuttings in a 50/50 mixture of coarse sand and peat-free potting mix, making sure the angled cut is just above soil level. It's best to grow them in modules to minimize root disturbance. Water and raise them under cover until the following spring.

Thinner roots

Plants with thinner roots, like anemones and hardy geraniums, need a slightly different approach. Select the large root from the parent plant and cut it into slightly longer lengths—between 3 and 5 in (8 and 13 cm).

Once trimmed, lay the cuttings horizontally on a mixture of 50/50 coarse sand and peat-free potting mix, press them in to ensure full contact with the soil, and then cover with either coarse sand or vermiculite. Give them a good water and pot them on next spring.

01

Lift and wash the roots

Lift the plant and wash the roots. Choose a root that is about a pencil thickness, cut it off, and replant the parent plant.

02

Cut into sections

Cut the root into small sections: between 2 and 4 in (5 and 10 cm) for thicker roots, and between 3 and 5 in (8 and 13 cm) for thinner roots. Cut one end at an angle.

03

Pot up

Lay thinner root cuttings horizontally on potting mix and press them in. Cover with coarse sand or vermiculite. Put thicker root cuttings in a 50/50 mixture of coarse sand and peat-free potting mix with the angled cut just above soil level. Water well.

Anemones are suitable for taking root cuttings using the technique for thinner roots.

Maintain

Your garden doesn't just look after itself. No matter how low maintenance it is, there will always be some sort of weekly, monthly, or annual maintenance to do. This is the magical part about gardening—nurturing it and watching it evolve through the seasons is a hugely rewarding process.

In this chapter, we'll look at some of the maintenance tasks I'd advise you to do every year, and I'll outline a range of seasonal jobs to keep your garden looking fantastic all year round. Maintaining your garden might feel overwhelming at first, but remember that there are time-management strategies you can adopt to keep on top of those routine gardening tasks throughout the seasons (see pp.28–33).

Yearly maintenance

Structures such as fences, patios, walls, and decks will need annual or even biannual maintenance to keep them looking good. Patios and paths can become slippery and hazardous, so late fall is the perfect time to give them some love before winter sets in. After the winter, I like to clean paths, steps, and patios again to look tidy for summer. It's a twice-a-year job to keep them looking well maintained year round. Your tools will also need some annual TLC.

Tools

Your trusty pruners, shears, and other favorite bladed tools experience some serious usage over the gardening season, so they do need some annual maintenance to keep them in good working order.

For bladed tools, I follow a simple step-by-step cleaning process. Start by cleaning any excess grime off the blades using clean, soapy water and a cloth. Wipe dry with a cloth. Use a medium- to fine-grade steel wool to remove any stubborn rust, dirt, or sap residue. Be careful around the sharp blade edges, working away from them, not toward them. Wipe the blades down using a clean, dry cloth to remove any rust sediment. Apply an oil to lubricate the blades: you can use flaxseed oil, camellia oil, general-purpose oil, vegetable oil, or WD40.

Clean bladed tools with steel wool to remove rust, dirt, or sap residue.

Fences

Every year, check for any rotten or broken fence panels and posts and replace them where necessary. If a fence post has rotted at the base, you can install a concrete spur to reinforce it rather than ripping the entire post and old concrete out of the ground. If you've painted your fence, reapply fence paint every couple of years, or, if you have opted for a long-life fence paint, you can usually stretch this out to every five years.

Patios

I recommend a twice-yearly maintenance schedule for patios—in spring to prepare for summer, and again in fall or winter to prevent them from becoming slip hazards.

Brush off and remove any debris like leaves and moss which can cause staining, especially on natural stones like limestone and sandstone. Rinse with a hose or light power wash (on its broadest fan setting). Spray the patio with a natural stone cleaner, allow it to absorb, and repeat. Don't let it dry out between first and second applications. Give the patio a final rinse-off.

On a dry day, I reseal the patio using a natural stone sealer, which stops moisture from getting in and protects the stone from frost damage and staining.

Decks

In fall and winter, decks can become treacherous and extremely slippery, unless, of course, you installed an anti-slip board. If you have a standard wooden deck, then you should apply the same principles of cleaning your patios and paths to decks.

Sweep off any leaves or dirt. Apply a nontoxic deck cleaning solution and let it soak in, scrub the deck down with a stiff-bristled brush to remove any harder grime or algae, and rinse off lightly with a power washer or hose. Then apply an anti-slip deck oil on a dry day and let it absorb into the wood. It will not only reduce the risk of slipping but also protect the wood.

These basic maintenance jobs will ensure you can keep using any deck spaces during fall and winter and prevent them becoming a slipping hazard.

Steps

Follow the same principles as you would to maintain your patio and paths. Remove any debris first, clean the area with a hose and stone cleaner if required, and finish off with a dusting of sand, especially in fall and winter when steps can become slippery. Check for any loose bricks or joints and replace and point if necessary.

Brickwork and walls

If you have brick or stone walls with mortar joints, it's worth giving them a check-over for any cracks. Point any loose joints to stop water from getting in and prevent frost damage over winter. It's important to check the stability and safety of walls and brick features all year round. If there are large cracks or the wall is starting to move, ask a professional about structural reinforcement.

Raised beds

Regularly check soil levels in raised beds, and apply a generous layer of mulch periodically if soil has depleted and the beds are looking low. Check for any loose gravel boards and secure them using timber screws. You can replace any rotten boards when required with a new piece of timber cut to size. If you've painted or varnished your raised bed, reapply the paint or varnish annually if needed.

Pergolas and other wooden structures

Check the wood for any signs of rot, cracking, splitting, or infection from pests, and replace if needed. Clean down and reapply a wood preserver, sealer, or paint every two years. Check for any loose joints and replace if required. Check the structural integrity: give the corner posts a little push to see if they are still sturdy. Also check that all plant supports, wires, and trellises are in good order, and tie in and maintain climbing plants to avoid overburdening the structure.

Compost bay

Check for any signs of rot or insect infestation in the wood, and replace pallets when they are no longer functional as a side wall. Ensure all the pallets are secure—if any screws are loose, add additional screws to strengthen the structure.

Water features

Turn off your water fountain in the fall to prevent damage from freezing temperatures. You probably only need to clean water features once every two years. In spring, remove your pond pump and clean all the internal filters using a brush and soapy water to ensure it's in good working order for spring and summer. You can drain the sump by pumping the water out with your pond pump, then give the area a good brush-down, removing any algae or dirt that's built up.

Clean any decorative stone around the water feature if it's covered with algae and grime. You can use soapy water or, if the stones are large enough, you can use a power washer. Check electrical connections are all in good working order. When you reconnect the pump to your above-ground water feature, make sure it's all resealed and watertight. Give the above-ground water feature the same cleaning treatment to remove any algae buildup or general grime.

Brick paths

Give brick paths a good brush-down using a stiff-bristled brush to remove any excess dirt or weeds in the joints. Then you have two options: either apply a stone cleaner with a sprayer and then wash off lightly with a hose, or apply a stone cleaner and then power wash if you're looking for a squeaky-clean finish. I recommend a very light power wash to avoid blowing out the brick faces and joints. You can forgo the stone cleaner if you prefer the natural, weathered look.

Check for any loose or broken bricks and repair where necessary. If the joints are cracked or blown in places, you can point those areas.

Paved paths

Clean paved paths with a stiff brush. If you jointed the paths with sand, sweep kiln-dried or sharp sand over the surface to refill any joints, which will prevent weeds and provide extra grip in winter. If your paths are joined with sand and cement or grout, check for joints that need pointing.

Tip

Apply a layer of kiln-dried or sharp sand to the surface of your paths to provide extra grip over winter.

Clean brick paths with a stiff brush to remove dirt or weeds in the joints.

Spring tasks

Spring has arrived and the garden starts to wake up from its winter dormancy. Spring bulbs are a much-welcome sight, adding color to the garden; trees are in bud and some put on a showstopping display of pink and white blossoms.

General seasonal tasks

These jobs can be completed throughout spring at any time.

Get planting! Now that spring is here, you can start planting out your favorite trees, shrubs, perennials, and climbers.

Be vigilant with weeds as they start to germinate, especially perennial nasties like ground elder, bindweed, and other spreaders. Start to build a habit of routinely weeding your garden. I leave a garden hoe in different spots and complete at least 20 minutes of weeding a day, especially during spring.

Sow seeds throughout spring, either directly into the ground or under cover, depending on the seed.

Opposite, clockwise from top left In spring, bulbs such as daffodils begin to pop up, and it's a good time to divide plants, such as this rudbeckia. Beautiful spring blossoms, such as *Prunus subhirtella* × 'Autumnalis', appear, and you can start to take tender plants back into the garden.

Keep on top of pest and disease control. As our gardens come to life, rain and warmer soil will encourage pests and diseases. Put in defenses such as slug and snail barriers, rabbit and squirrel fencing, and bird netting; spray plants with organic insecticides and pesticides; and prepare to get physical by removing unwanted pests from the garden. Be especially vigilant with your greenhouse plants. As the greenhouse warms, it creates a perfect humid environment for pests and diseases to thrive.

Start watering newly planted trees, shrubs, perennials, and container plants.

Keep checking greenhouse temperatures, ventilate during warm days, heat during cold snaps if you're growing tender plants, and consider shading solutions for the summer.

Dig up and divide perennials. Dividing perennials is a job I prefer to do in the fall, but spring is also a great time to do it (see p.155).

Top up your raised beds to replace soil that has washed away and add nutrients that have been depleted.

Make sure rainwater-harvesting systems like rain barrels and troughs are connected to gutters to collect water for the garden.

Start mowing your lawn again with regular trims. It might be worth having the mower serviced as we head into the new growing season.

Plant up containers for your spring and summer displays.

Early spring tasks

Early spring is full of promise: the garden is greening up and the soil is starting to warm, making it the perfect time to start planting and sowing certain crops. The weather can still be unpredictable, though, and we haven't escaped the risk of frost, so be cautious with planting out any tender plants.

Take care of your borders. If you have left your borders for winter and refrained from cutting back herbaceous perennials, now is a great time to clear your borders to allow for new growth to flourish. If you didn't get around to it, there's still time to give your borders a good mulch before spring gets into full flow.

Start installing plant supports for tall flowering perennials toward the back of your borders, or for shrubs that tend to flop (see p.109).

Plant up summer bulbs like gladioli, lilies, and oxalis.

Cut back dogwoods and other shrubs known for their colorful foliage and stems, as the best color is produced on new stems. Dogwood (*Cornus*) and other plants like elder (*Sambucus*) and smoke tree (*Cotinus*) can tolerate hard pruning. Save the stems for hardwood cuttings (see p.157). You can also create a hedge using the dogwood cuttings.

Layer shrubs like dogwoods, buddleia, and hydrangeas to create new plants for next year (see p.154).

Layer a shrub by pinning down a shoot until it forms roots.

Take basal cuttings now from plants like achilleas, delphiniums, and lupins (see p.155). You can also take cuttings from dahlia tubers once a few shoots appear.

Mulch your roses and feed in early spring to give them a boost for summer.

Order and plant bare-root roses, shrubs, and trees. Early spring is your last chance to do this until fall.

Plant a hedge from bare-root hedging plants. This is your last chance until fall or winter because later on you will only be able to purchase more expensive pot-grown plants. See pp.138–141 for how to plant a hedge.

Prune back your hydrangeas to the first pair of healthy buds. Some hydrangeas, such as panicled varieties, flower on new wood, while others, such as mopheads and lacecaps, flower on old wood, so it's best to check which type you have before pruning.

Lay sod, and repair and seed lawns. Now is a good time to be getting your lawn in order. See pp.152–153 for how to lay sod.

Prune and repot tender plants like pelargoniums and other tender perennials you overwintered in the greenhouse. Keeping a nice, open structure, prune back stems aggressively by a third to the nearest set of new buds. This will promote plenty of flowering vigor for the year ahead.

Take softwood cuttings of herbaceous perennials and shrubs like catmints (*Nepeta*), salvias, and pelargoniums, as well as shrubs like hydrangea (see p.156).

Prepare raised beds and borders for direct sowing of flowers and vegetable crops. Add some fresh compost or mushroom compost to reinvigorate your beds for sowing—2 to 3in (5 to 8cm) of quality mulch will give your plants a great start to life. Rake it over to create a fine tilth ready for sowing.

Move evergreen shrubs if they have outgrown the space or are simply in the wrong position. I prefer to do this in spring, because moving in winter is more risky. The plant can't replace water lost through its leaves because of cold winds and frosty conditions. You can also move plants in fall (see p.178). Refer to p.125 for how to move plants.

Opposite, clockwise from top left Growth starts to emerge in abundance, so prune back hydrangeas, take softwood cuttings of catmint, sow seeds, and take basal cuttings of delphiniums.

CARING FOR ROSES

Be on the lookout for black spot on roses, and spray any infected leaves with fungicide. Remove any fallen infected leaves and dispose of them, either by burning or in your city's yard waste collection. Yard waste is a good option as heat is used to burn off any pests and diseases. Don't compost the leaves because you could potentially recycle the disease and spread it across the rest of your garden if the compost heap hasn't generated enough heat.

Treat aphids and other pests with an organic pesticide or a soapy water mix, or physically remove them.

Mid-spring tasks

Mid-spring is one of the most stunning periods in the gardening calendar: the season is in full flow, the garden is starting to come to life, and temperatures are rising. Tulips are taking a front-row seat in many gardens, alongside other gorgeous spring-flowering bulbs. Mid-spring can still be unpredictable in some places, with April showers and the chance of frost.

Take care of your roses. Watch out for black spot disease, aphids, and other pests (see box left).

Check that water pumps and fountains are in good working order and turn them back on.

Clean your patios and paths (see pp.163, 165) and pull up the weeds—this will ensure the bones of your garden are given a glow-up for the summer.

Start feeding your lawn with lawn fertilizer.

Watch out for self-seeders of trees, shrubs, perennials, and grasses. While I encourage self-seeding, there will be times when plants are simply in the wrong place, so remove where necessary and either replant in a new location or add to the compost heap.

Prune clematis (see p.186).

Stay vigilant for pests and diseases on roses, and treat them appropriately.

Start feeding your lawn with fertilizer.

Plant container-grown plants in the ground. Bare-root stock will no longer be available, but container-grown plants can be planted all year round.

Prune back winter- and early-spring-flowering shrubs, such as forsythia and sarcococca, once they have finished flowering. Either simply cut off the spent blooms to tidy up the plant or prune back by one-third to reinvigorate the plant with fresh, new growth.

Tie in shoots of vigorous climbers like wisteria and clematis, and any new growth of climbing and rambling roses, to plant supports and structures.

Finish lifting and dividing summer-flowering herbaceous perennials, especially if you would like them to flower this year (see p.155).

Pot on the softwood cuttings you may have taken earlier because their root systems will have started to establish by now.

Start to acclimatize dahlias you started in late winter (see p.185) to external temperatures by taking them outside during the day.

Remove spent blooms from spring bulbs that have gone over to ensure they put the energy back into the bulb for next year, instead of making seeds.

Late spring tasks

Late spring is one of my favorite times in the gardening year, when gardens explode into color. The warmer temperatures and longer daylight hours make it perfect for plants to thrive and for gardeners to embrace their blooming gardens.

With the soil warmed up, weeds will be starting to germinate and the spring weeding battle starts.

Do some serious pruning. Prune back select herbaceous perennials, such as catmints (*Nepeta*), heleniums, and rudbeckias, by at least one-third of the overall size. This will delay their flowering until later on in the season, ultimately extending summer interest.

Thin out borders. By this point, your work from the fall and winter is starting to be visible with all the vigorous top growth. You may need to thin out borders in places to allow room for other plants to come through.

Prune evergreen hedges, if necessary. Birds may be nesting, so be mindful of any wildlife. Now is the time to lightly trim any topiary.

Plant out dahlias and other tender perennials once all risk of frost has passed.

Remove all frost protection from tender plants ready for summer. Check the weather forecast—late frosts are still a potential threat.

Move tender plants that overwintered in a greenhouse or conservatory into the garden.

Pot on softwood cuttings.

Sow seeds of some of your favorite perennials directly outside. Refer to p.133 for some of my favorites.

Clear out spring container displays to make way for the summer show.

Mow new lawns. Providing there's at least 2–3 in (5–7.5 cm) of growth, lawns you sowed earlier in spring are now ready for their first cut. Set the mower blades at their highest cutting height for the first mow, and then gradually reduce the height for subsequent cuts.

Meteorological summer June 1–August 31

Summer tasks

By summer, there are bountiful blooms to enjoy, and the sound of pollinators buzzing around is something we just want to bottle up and hold onto forever. The summer season is the best month for color, but drought occurs more frequently, and it can be a trying season for plants.

General seasonal tasks

These jobs can be completed throughout summer at any time.

Keep on top of routine watering for beds, borders, and especially containers, which can dry out quickly. Watering in the morning or evening is best.

Mow lawns regularly during the summer. Don't reduce any more than 25 percent of the overall height for a healthy lawn.

Feed established lawns with an appropriate lawn fertilizer to reinvigorate them over summer. Established lawns can benefit from watering, but they are resilient, and even if they turn brown, they will green back up again.

Opposite, clockwise from top left Summer is the season of ongoing maintenance, ensuring your yard looks its best: trim hedges, clear water features of built-up algae, keep on top of deadheading, and start your routine watering.

Water new lawns regularly during hot spells to stop them from drying out.

Keep on top of weeding. Weeds are at their most prolific, so hoe out annual weeds while they are still small and don't get the chance to set seed.

Deadhead! Now is the time to keep on top of deadheading to extend your summer display—the more you deadhead, the more blooms you will be rewarded with, and this especially applies to roses and dahlias.

Keep water features and ponds topped up and clear any algae buildup to allow light in for healthy plants to thrive and to encourage biodiversity.

Watch out for pests and diseases in the garden, conservatory, greenhouse, or cold frame. A sticky residue and defoliation are signs of mealybug, spider mites, and aphids.

Shade and ventilate greenhouses. Make a habit of opening up the doors when hot temperatures are forecast. Damping down the greenhouse with a hose is also a good tactic for cooling the environment.

Leave food and water out for the birds. They are a vital asset and contributor to a thriving ecosystem. The summer period can be trying for birds: long, hot, dry spells can cause core water sources to dry up, and earthworms tend to bury themselves deeper, making it harder for birds to forage.

Trim hedges as they will put on a fair amount of growth during the summer season.

Continue potting up softwood cuttings you took in spring and place them out of direct sunlight to prevent scorching and drying out.

Plan for vacations. Arrange cover while you're away for watering plants, mowing the lawn, and ventilating the greenhouse.

Early summer tasks

Early summer can be very hot, so be prepared for periods of drought. Keep on top of routine watering and maintenance at this time—they can hugely impact the success of your gardening season.

Tie in climbing and rambling roses as they start to put on vigorous growth, and prune out any dead, diseased, or damaged parts.

Cut back early-flowering perennials such as Balkan clary 'Caradonna' (*Salvia nemorosa* 'Caradonna'), catmints (*Nepeta*), and hardy geraniums to promote a second flush of flowering in late summer.

Fill any bare patches in your borders with pot-grown plants from a nursery to ensure you have a complete border throughout the remainder of summer. If they are temporary plants, you can mark out these spots with canes to indicate where you have gaps for fall or spring planting.

Tie in climbing and rambling roses.

Apply and renew mulches. To use water more sparingly, a good tactic is to water the garden generously and then apply a thick layer of mulch to help trap moisture in and reduce the need for watering later in summer.

Prune mature deciduous shrubs that have finished flowering to promote a potential second flush of flowering and lush, new growth to remain leafy over summer, and maintain flowering vigor for next year.

Prune back overgrown lilacs once they have finished flowering. They respond well to a hard pruning to 2 ft (60 cm) above soil level, which will provide you with an abundance of fresh foliage. This fresh growth will bear the new flowering vigor for next season.

Propagate climbers like wisteria, clematis, and honeysuckle by layering (see p.154). The rooting stems will be ready to sever from the main stem and pot on during fall.

Remove spent leaves and flowers of hellebores. By now, they are usually looking pretty tired and are potentially infected with leaf spot, so it's best to remove the leaves and make way for the new growth coming from the crown of the plant.

Prune back spent blooms of euphorbias. Wear gloves as the sap can be an irritant to the skin. *Euphorbia characias* flowers on biennial stems, and it should be cut down to the base of the plant after flowering. The new stems will provide the flowering vigor the following year. Deciduous types can be cut down to ground level after flowering in the fall.

Plant out summer bulbs like lilies and cannas that you have grown under cover.

Midsummer tasks

By midsummer, our gardens have reached a crescendo, with flowers popping up everywhere, and it's time to take stock of all of the hard graft you put into the garden during winter and spring.

Cut back finished perennials to promote healthy new growth. You may get the bonus of a second flush, or you can simply keep the spent blooms to enjoy as structural interest during fall and winter.

Give your roses a good midsummer feed with a liquid seaweed, tomato food, or rose food. This will promote flowering vigor well into late summer and fall.

Prune stone-fruit trees prone to silver-leaf disease, such as plums, apricots, and cherries, now as there are fewer fungal spores in the air. Prune seed-based fruits, like apples, pears, and quince, when they are dormant in winter (see p.183).

Remove suckers and unwanted growth from the base of trees and shrubs. Roses and certain trees such as mountain ash are prone to producing suckers. By removing them, you will encourage the plant to focus its growing energy where you want it to.

Take semi-ripe cuttings of certain plants, such as rosemary and lavender. Use wood that has grown this year and has almost turned from green to brown (see p.157).

Divide bearded iris once the blooms have faded (see p.155).

Remove small, lateral dahlia buds to put energy back into the central, large bud on the main stem and promote larger, single flowers.

Give container displays a liquid seaweed or tomato food to promote further flowering.

Deadhead and remove spent blooms of buddleia.

Late summer tasks

Late summer can be a hot period with high temperatures and days that are still long, making it a lovely month to enjoy the garden. Droughts can be quite common, so watering in the mornings or evenings starts to become more frequent, and weeds and pests can be prolific, given the ideal conditions for them.

Prune climbing and rambling roses to shape, or keep the rose hips for fall and winter interest.

Prune your wisteria to keep it relatively in check, pruning back to five buds from the main stem and tying in any stems you want to keep.

Collect seed from some of your favorite perennials and store them in a paper bag in a cool, dry, dark place ready for sowing in spring.

Deadhead and remove spent blooms of buddleia if you want to avoid them self-seeding everywhere in the garden.

Take cuttings from tender perennials like salvias so you have a supply in case they don't make it through the winter (see p.156).

Take semi-ripe cuttings of penstemons because they don't take to division very well and are very easy plants to grow from cuttings (see p.157).

Cut back herbaceous perennials—those with nonwoody stems, such as hardy geraniums and *Nepeta*—that have flopped over lawns, because they can shade and kill the grass below. This will also help shape them for a final flurry of foliage heading into fall.

Prune summer-flowering jasmine after flowering. Alternatively, you can leave it until late winter (see p.185) or early spring.

TAKE PHOTOS

Take plenty of photos and videos of your garden during its peak, so you can plan for next year. Having images will allow you to assess gaps in your borders and the structural bones of your garden. It will help you identify ways to improve the rhythm of your space by bringing in more color and form with your planting.

Meteorological fall September 1–November 30

Fall tasks

When it comes to favorite seasons, fall tops the list for me. The colors, light, and natural beauty found in the garden and elsewhere outdoors are truly breathtaking. Beyond its visual appeal, fall is also one of the busiest seasons for gardeners. It's the ideal time for planning, planting, and preparing the garden for next year's display.

General seasonal tasks

These jobs can be completed throughout fall at any time.

Continue collecting seeds of your favorite perennials, remembering to leave some for the birds.

Plant new trees, shrubs, and perennials. See pp.142–149 for full step-by-step instructions on how to plant trees, shrubs, and perennials.

Order and plant bare-root roses, shrubs, and trees for a fraction of the price of potted plants.

Clean out your greenhouse and wash the glass to allow maximum light exposure inside.

Opposite, clockwise from top left
Clear out greenhouse gutters to channel rainwater; collect and compost plant material; plant new trees, shrubs, and perennials; and continue deadheading.

Continue weeding and tidying your beds and borders. Keep on top of perennial weeds and tidy your borders, removing any collapsed, soggy plant material.

Store hoses under cover, including standard garden hoses, drip fed, and seep hoses, to protect them from freezing and splitting.

Clear out gutters and drains—remove fallen leaves and other debris to prevent clogging.

Maintain structures such as raised beds, sheds, arches, and pergolas (see p.164). Repair if necessary and reapply a wood preserver to protect them in winter.

Plant spring bulbs such as *Iris reticulata*, *Narcissus*, snowdrops (*Galanthus*), crocus, and grape hyacinth (*Muscari*). See pp.150–151 for how to plant bulbs.

Mulch your garden. This is best done in the fall before winter sets in, although your garden would benefit from being mulched periodically, once in fall and again in spring (see box on p.178).

Build your compost heaps, given the excess plant material available in the garden. See pp.116–117 for step-by-step instructions on how to build your own compost bay.

Maintain hard landscaping features such as walls, patios, paths, and steps—refer to the maintenance routines on pp.162–165.

Give your tools some TLC—see the maintenance section on p.162.

Build hard landscaping features such as paths, patios, fencing, and other structures before winter sets in (see p.43).

THE MERITS OF MULCHING

The reason mulching is so good for your soil health in the fall is down to a number of factors. It protects your soil and all the beneficial microorganisms over harsh winters, helps insulate the roots of your favorite plants, and suppresses weeds. It will also break down gradually over winter, improving soil structure and fertility, ready for spring.

I recommend applying a thick layer of mulch—2 to 3 in (5 to 7.5 cm) of quality mulch is a good rule of thumb to work toward. If you have a large garden or sizable borders, mulching can sometimes feel overwhelming and labor intensive. In this scenario, a mulching schedule can be helpful. Break the space down into more achievable areas, and thoroughly mulch smaller spaces periodically as opposed to laying a thin layer across all of the areas.

Early fall tasks

During early fall, the most significant noticeable difference is the days getting shorter. The following tasks are best done now, while the ground is still warm and temperatures are relatively mild.

Deadhead late-flowering perennials, such as roses and buddleia. There is still plenty of life with late-flowering perennials, so if you keep on top of deadheading, you can encourage some extra blooms and color during early fall.

Sow a new lawn or wildflower meadow. Early fall is a fantastic time to do this because the ground is still warm and conditions are optimal for germination. It also gives the new lawn or meadow time to establish itself before spring, giving everything a great head start.

Trim conifer hedges such as yew to control height and keep them tidy during winter.

Mid-fall tasks

By mid-fall, the season is in full swing, and that is reflected in trees dropping their leaves and the increasing frequency of rain showers.

As temperatures start to drop, there are a number of jobs that should be completed while the ground isn't frozen and before the weather takes a turn. It's also an optimal time to protect plants and prepare the garden for winter.

Prune lavender. By now, it will be well and truly over, and this is really the last month for pruning. It's straightforward to do: grab a cluster of the spent flowers and prune back soft, green wood to within ½ to 1¼ in (1–3 cm) of the old wood. Don't prune back to the old hardwood as this can potentially kill the plant—just make sure there is still some fresh growth on top. The aim is to create a neat, dome-like structure that will look tidy over winter. Save some of the spent flowering stems to bring into the house for their scent.

Move plants that are in the wrong place (see p.125). The good news is that most plants are movable and now is the time to do it while the ground is still warm. Some plants, however, really don't like their roots being disturbed and will suffer from transplant shock, so it's important to research the plant before you move it.

Keep lawns free from fallen leaves which can block out vital light required for photosynthesis, promote fungal diseases, and encourage moss growth, which can be detrimental to sustaining a healthy lawn.

Bring in tender plants now the days and nights are getting colder, with a risk of frosty mornings, to protect them over winter. Insulate or heat your greenhouse to protect any tender plants overnight—it is perfect for storing plants, or a conservatory is also a good spot.

Tie in plants. Winds start to pick up by mid-fall, so make sure you have adequate supports for any climbing plants. If you've tied plants to trellises or other supports using garden twine, then usually you will need to refresh the ties because they will rot and decompose. This is a quick, routine job but definitely worthwhile—there's nothing worse than seeing a beautiful climber ripped off a wall and damaged by stormy weather.

Take hardwood cuttings from shrubs and herbs such as lavender, rosemary, and thyme (see p.157). The cuttings can be planted directly in the ground or potted up in containers to grow on in a greenhouse or cold frame.

Opposite, above right, and right
Prune back your lavender, creating a nice, dome-like mound for winter. Bring in any tender plants to protect them over winter. Mid-fall is a good time to take hardwood cuttings.

Late fall tasks

By late fall, our gardens are slowly heading for dormancy over winter, and the weather has well and truly turned, with an increase in rain, wind, and potentially snow. Depending on your region, there's a chance of frost.

As temperatures continue to drop, this is really the last chance to complete certain garden tasks before the cold winter season kicks in.

Prune shrub roses—wind rock can damage the root system of larger shrubs and trees because of the stress of continuous movement caused by the prevailing winds. You can reduce the overall size of shrub roses by 25 percent to keep the shrub more compact and neater over winter and less susceptible to wind damage. For trees, you could mitigate wind rock by installing stakes (see pp.143–144).

Plant spring bulbs, such as daffodils (*Narcissus*), crocus, alliums, snowdrops, irises, hyacinths, tulips, and fritillaries (see pp.150–151).

Turn off water fountains if you live in an area prone to freezing temperatures to prevent them from being damaged by ice. This will also save you money on your energy bills.

Collect leaves to make leaf mold (see box right).

Left, from top It's time to get planting some of your favorite spring-flowering bulbs. Don't forget to turn off water features to protect pumps from being damaged over winter.

MAKE LEAF MOLD

Leaf mold is a great soil improver and can be used for seed sowing. Mix it with a little sand and compost to make a potting mix.

I make leaf mold every year and the process is simple: collect fallen leaves from trees such as beech, hornbeam, oak, elm, birch, and hazel. Avoid strappy leaves from laurel, horse chestnut, magnolia, and sycamore, because they decompose more slowly and need shredding first. Avoid using leaves from busy residential streets, because they can pick up toxins from vehicle exhausts.

Store your collected leaves either in a composter to break down or in a trash can or trash bags, but remember to poke holes in the bottom so moisture can get out and air can get in.

The decomposition process usually takes between one and two years. Sometimes leaves break down more quickly, but a general rule of thumb is 18 months. When ready to use, it's a dark, soft material with some half-decomposed leaves.

Opposite, clockwise from top left To make leaf mold, collect fallen leaves in your garden. Drill holes in the bottom of a trash can. Add the leaves and leave to decompose for one to two years. When ready, the leaf mold will be dark and have a crumbly texture.

Winter tasks

Winter has arrived, and it's a magical season for many reasons. Plants are lightly dusted with morning frosts; cobwebs sparkle; and the bright, crystal-blue skies are a delight. The garden begins to enter dormancy, and your core structural trees, shrubs, and ornamental grasses take center stage, while everything else gradually fades around them.

General seasonal tasks

These jobs can be completed throughout winter at any time.

Continue to clear your borders, removing any soggy plant material from herbaceous perennials. Plants like crocosmias and hostas will produce a slimy mess when they decompose, which can suffocate and damage the plant if it's left to rot in situ. Remove and compost.

Continue mulching. If the ground isn't completely frozen and you haven't already mulched your beds and borders, spread a generous amount of well-rotted manure or compost to give your plants vital nutrients before spring (see box on p.178).

Opposite, clockwise from top left
Winter is where the work really happens: get mulching your beds and borders, plant bare-root roses, create a new hedge, and maintain ornamental grasses.

Plant bare-root plants. It's still prime time for planting bare-root trees, shrubs, roses, and various fruit bushes. Take advantage of bare-root season and get some planted before early spring.

Plant deciduous hedges, such as hornbeam, beech, and hazel. See pp.138–141 for how to plant a hedge.

Check plants for pests and diseases, and treat them with organic pesticides or physical controls.

Check overwintering bulbs and tubers for any sign of rot over winter, and discard or add any rotten ones to the compost heap.

Clean pots to get them ready for the spring display.

Continue to check patios, paths, and decks to ensure they haven't built up algae and become hazardous to walk on—sand and clean them if necessary (see pp.163, 165).

Comb through evergreen grasses to remove dead blades and reinvigorate the plant.

Continue weeding perennial weeds and keep on top of border maintenance.

Prune fruit trees and deciduous shrubs to shape them and to improve overall plant health (see p.186).

Protect plants from snow and harsh frosts—even tough shrubs and trees can suffer, so if you have any particular favorites, it's worth protecting them with burlap.

Ensure you feed birds in the colder weather and keep baths topped up with fresh water.

Keep off frosted or wet lawns to limit any potential damage.

Early winter tasks

Early winter can be a quiet time for gardening because of the cold weather, as well as the timing of festivities and the holiday season.

Take root cuttings of perennials, such as oriental poppies, *Verbascum*, anemones, and acanthus (see p.158). Plant out in spring.

Take hardwood cuttings of shrubs and trees (see p.157).

Sow early ornamentals like snapdragons and pelargoniums to give them a head start.

Lift and move deciduous shrubs and trees now so they have time to settle back down before spring arrives (see p.125).

Order summer-flowering bulbs and tubers like dahlias, lilies, and gladioli to make sure you secure your favorites before spring.

Browse plant catalogs for inspiration, and note what seeds you want to sow and plants you want to add to the garden next year.

Check newly planted shrubs and trees for any signs of wind rock or loosening around the base of the plant. If they feel loose, firm them in again with your foot.

Remove hellebore leaves infected with leaf spot, if you've not done so already, to allow more light for the newly emerging leaves. This is your last chance before hellebores start flowering in late winter or early spring.

Check hellebores and remove any leaves infected with leaf spot.

Midwinter tasks

Midwinter and the new year are an exciting time for gardeners because they bring hope and optimism for the season ahead. That said, the colder weather can put people off venturing into the garden.

Prune your wisteria. I usually do this job once the leaves have dropped. Prune each side shoot back to within two buds from the main stem (see also p.186).

Check tree ties and tree stakes, ensuring they are secure given the likelihood of high winds in winter.

Order herbaceous perennials from online nurseries so you are ready to start planting in early spring. It's worth getting a preorder in even if they won't arrive until spring, because stock levels deplete quickly. You wouldn't want to miss out on those "must-have" plants.

Late winter tasks

Late winter can be hit or miss. It can be very cold, but there can be mild spells, which give us a glimmer of spring to come. Spring bulbs are starting to emerge and our gardens are slowly awakening.

Feed hedges, shrubs, and trees with a slow-release fertilizer to give them a vital shot of nutrients during late winter and heading into spring.

Cut back deciduous grasses to 4 in (10 cm) above ground level.

Begin to sow hardy annuals. If you're a lover of chiles, as I am, you can sow them under cover now using a heated propagator or on a warm windowsill.

Prune back shrub, rambling, and climbing roses. You can do this in late winter or early spring, but I prefer to do it in late winter (see p.186).

Prune side shoots of wisteria to two buds from the main stem.

Prune back buddleia and other deciduous shrubs. You can prune back by at least two-thirds to reinvigorate the plant for the following year.

Prune clematis (see p.186).

Top-dress shrubs in containers to replace soil depleted during winter.

Order bulbs in the green—bulbs that have been potted up and grown on by nurseries. The advantage of buying bulbs in the green is that you know they are alive and healthy as their leaves are showing, and you're not waiting an entire season to see if they show. It also allows you to space them well, as you can see the size of the plants, not just the bulb.

Start growing dahlia tubers under cover on a warm windowsill or in a heated greenhouse.

Order plenty of potting mix ready for sowing seeds, planting out in spring, container planting, and more.

Prune summer-flowering jasmine if you didn't prune after flowering in late summer (see p.175). You can prune back to strong lateral stems now or in early spring, because the plant flowers on new growth.

Prune back tender perennials like pelargoniums by one-third to reinvigorate the plant ahead of the new season. Leftover material can be used for cuttings.

CHOP AND DROP

Chop and drop is one of the most sustainable ways to mulch your garden. I tend to leave all of my herbaceous perennials and grasses over winter for structure—I love to see the frost formations on the plants and seed heads, which provide vital food for birds and habitat for other wildlife during the colder months.

In late winter, I cut everything except core shrubs and trees almost to ground level and leave the plant trimmings to mulch into the ground naturally where they fall—hence the name chop and drop. Not only is this a hugely efficient way to mulch your beds and borders, it saves you time and money because you don't have to buy mulch and lug it into the garden.

I have used the chop and drop method for almost a decade now, and I've found it to be a game-changer in the way I garden. In terms of self-sufficiency and zero-waste gardening, chop and drop is a perfect example of nothing coming in and nothing being removed—it's 100 percent sustainable and the most natural way to mulch your garden.

1. Remove any diseased or pest-infested plant material to prevent it from spreading in the border.
2. Remove seed heads of prolific self-seeders if you don't want them to spread everywhere.
3. Cut down plants in increments of 3–5 in (7.5–13 cm) so you create an even mulch.
4. Spread the mulch evenly using a garden hoe to cover any bare soil.

Use a cordless hedge trimmer to speed up the time it takes to chop and drop.

Resources

Calculating materials

Subbase

bullimores.net/mot-type-1-calculator/

Paving

pavingdirect.com/info/patio-paving-calculators/

Bricks

jewson.co.uk/material-calculators/brick

Pruning clematis

General guidance

rhs.org.uk/plants/clematis/pruning-guide

Group 1

rhs.org.uk/plants/clematis/group-one-pruning-guide

Group 2

rhs.org.uk/plants/clematis/group-two-pruning-guide

Group 3

rhs.org.uk/plants/clematis/group-three-pruning-guide

Roses

Marriott, Michael, *Roses: An Inspirational Guide to Choosing and Growing the Best Roses*, DK, 2022.

General pruning guidance

rhs.org.uk/plants/roses/pruning-guide

Pruning climbing roses

rhs.org.uk/plants/roses/climbing/pruning-guide

Pruning rambling roses

rhs.org.uk/plants/roses/rambler/pruning-guide

Pruning shrub roses

rhs.org.uk/plants/roses/shrub/pruning-guide

Pruning wisteria

rhs.org.uk/plants/wisteria/pruning-guide

Pruning fruit trees

rhs.org.uk/fruit/apples/pruning-new-trees

Pruning trees and shrubs

rhs.org.uk/plants/types/trees/trees-shrubs-light-pruning

rhs.org.uk/advice/beginners-guide/pruning-plants/pruning-shrubs

Plant identification apps

PictureThis—Plant identifier

PlantNet—Plant identification

RHS Grow—Plant and garden care

Seeds

Burpee

burpee.com

Index

A
access 18
access lighting 100
acidic soil plants 136
alkaline soil plants 136
alternatives to concrete and mortar 43
angle grinders 63
aspect 14–15

B
ballast 42
bare-root rose planting 146–47, 168, 177
basal cuttings 155, 168
beds and borders
  design considerations 88–89
  edging 89
  ground preparation 89
  maintenance 164, 167, 168, 171, 174, 177, 183
  raised beds 89–92, 164, 167
benches 99
birds, feeding 173, 183
blockwork 82
borders *see* beds and borders
boundaries, types 47
bricks
  how to build a brick path 68–71
  how to build a retaining wall 82–87
  paths 53
buddleia 167, 175, 185
budget 26–27, 53
building
  checklist 37
  concrete and mortar 42–43
  learning skills 37
  seasons 43
  tools 39, 40–41
bulbs
  how to plant bulbs 150–51
  maintenance 171, 183
  ordering 184, 185
  planting, 164, 174, 180
  suggested choices 133

C
cement 43
cement mixers 41
chop and drop 185
clematis 170, 171, 174, 185
climbers
  maintenance 171, 174, 175, 184
  propagation 174
  suggested choices 133
  ties and twine 179
color
  color wheel and palette 123
  repetition 122
compost 114–15, 164, 177
  how to build a compost bay 116–17
concrete 42–45
concrete pumps 45
conservation areas 20
construction *see* building
containers *see* pots
coping bricks/stones 87
corms, suggested choices 133
corners, squaring 59
Corten steel 102
cottage gardens 128
cuttings
  basal 155, 168
  hardwood 157, 179, 184
  root 158
  semi-ripe 157, 175
  softwood 156, 168
cutting slabs 63

D
dahlias 171, 175, 185
damp-proof course 14
deadheading 173, 178
decks 163, 183
delivery of materials 18–19
design *see* planning
dining tables and chairs 98–99
disease control 167, 173, 183
dividing plants 155, 167, 171
dogwoods 168
downlighting 101
drainage
  assessment during planning 14
  fall rates 60, 61
  patios and paths 54–55
drain clearing 177
driveway lighting 101
dumpsters 19

E
euphorbias 174
exposed area plants 135

F
fall maintenance 177–81
fall rates 60, 61
fences
  boundaries 47
  maintenance 163
  slatted fence project 48–51
focal points 93, 100
footings *see* foundations
formal gardens 128
form, planting 121
foundations
  patios and paths 54, 60–62, 69
  steps 76
  walls 83–84
frost protection 179, 183

G
garden screening 81
grasses
  laying sod 152–53
  suggested choices 133
gravel gardens 128
gravel paths 53, 55
greenhouses 167, 173, 177
gutters 177

H

hardwood cuttings 157, 179, 184
hazel lattice project 110–13
heavy clay plants 135
hedging
- boundaries 47
- feeding 184
- maintenance 171, 173, 178
- planting project 138–40, 168, 183

height of plants 131
hellebores 174, 184
herbaceous perennials
- dividing 155, 167, 171
- maintenance 174, 175
- planting 148–49, 177
- suggested choices 133

hori hori 41
hoses 177
hydrangeas 168

I

irises 175

J

jasmine 175, 185
jungle gardens 129

L

lattice supports 109–13
lavender 178
lawns
- how to lay sod 152–53
- maintenance 168, 170, 173, 178
- mowing 167, 171, 173
- sowing 178

layering 154, 168, 174
leaf mold 180
legal requirements 20–21
levels and layout 16–17
lighting 19, 100–101
lilacs 174
long-handled iron bar 40

M

maintenance
- beds and borders 164, 167, 168, 171
- brickwork and walls 164
- compost 164
- decks 163
- design considerations 11
- fall 177–81
- fences 163
- hedging 171, 173
- paths 164, 183
- patios 163, 170, 183
- pergolas 164
- plants and seasons 131
- raised beds 164
- spring 167–71
- steps 163
- summer 173–75
- tools 39, 162
- water features 164, 170, 173
- winter 183–85

materials
- bed edging 88
- delivery 18–19
- outdoor structures 93
- patios and paths 54–56
- recycling and upcycling 27
- walls 81

mattocks 41
membrane installation 54, 60, 69
microclimates 16
mood boards 11
moonlighting 101
mortar 42–45
movement, plants 121
moving plants 125, 168, 178, 184
mowing 167, 171, 173
mulching 174, 177, 178, 183, 185

N

naturalistic gardens 129
neighbors 21
new gardens, understanding space 11

O

obelisks 109
odd number planting 122
outdoor structures
- maintenance 164, 177
- overview 93

P

paths
- design considerations 52–53
- foundations 54, 69
- how to build a brick path 68–71
- maintenance 164, 183
- materials 54–56
- paving styles 56–57

patios
- design considerations 52–53
- fall rates 60–61
- foundations 54, 60–62
- how to build a patio 58–61
- maintenance 163, 170, 183
- materials 54–56
- sealing 63

pavers 55
paving styles 56–57
penstemons 175
perennials
- dividing 155, 167, 171
- maintenance 174, 175, 185
- planting 148–49, 177
- suggested choices 133

pergolas 93
- how to build a pergola 94–97
- maintenance 164

permeability, patios and paths 54–55
pest control 167, 173, 183
photo records 175
planning
- access and services 18–19
- aspect 14–15
- basic considerations 11
- budgets 26–27
- drainage 14

focal points 93, 100
ground-based plans 25
legal requirements 20–21
microclimates 16
photo records 175
planting design 121–23, 131
project plans 30
scaled plans 24–25
seasons 31
soil type 12–13
time management 28–31
topography 16–17
use and function 11
well-being 33
planting
bulbs 150–51, 164, 174, 180
design considerations 121–23, 131
grouping and layering 124
hedges 138–40, 168, 183
herbaceous perennials 148–49, 177
impact 124–25
seasonal interest 125
seasons and timing 31
shrubs 145–47, 177, 183
styles 128–29
tools 39, 41
trees 142–44, 177
plants
choosing 130–31
cuttings 155–58
dividing 155, 171
existing mature specimens 27
frost protection 179, 183
layering 154, 168
moving 125, 168, 178, 184
right plant, right place 131, 134–35
suggested choices 133
plant supports 109
pointing 64, 72, 79, 87
ponds 103, 107
post hole diggers 40
posts, placing 49–50, 91, 95–96
pots
feeding 175
planting up 167
size and impact 124
top-dressing 185
winter maintenance 183
priorities 30
project plans 30
property lines, ownership 20
pruning 168, 170–71, 174, 178, 180, 183, 184
pumps, water features 107

Q

quotations 27

R

rainwater-harvesting 167
raised beds 89, 164, 167
how to build a raised bed 90–92
ramblers, suggested choices 133
ramps, design considerations 73
recycling 27, 114
renting tools 39, 45
repetition, planting 122
retaining walls *see* walls
rhythm, planting 122, 175
right plant, right place 131, 134–35
root cuttings 158
roses
bare-root planting 146–47, 168, 177
feeding 174
pest and disease monitoring 170
pruning 175, 180, 184

S

screening 81
seasons
fall maintenance 177–81
maintenance 131
planning 31
planting impact 125
spring maintenance 167–71
summer maintenance 173–75
winter maintenance 183–85
seating 98–99
security lighting 100
seed collection 175, 177
self-seeding 170
semi-ripe cuttings 157, 175
services location 19
shade, aspect 14–15
shade-loving plants 134
shrubs
feeding 184
moving 125, 168, 184
planting 145–47, 177, 183
pruning 168, 170–71, 174, 175, 180
suggested choices 133
silhouetting 101
slopes 16–17
sod laying 152–53
sofas 98
softwood cuttings 156, 168
soil
pH 12
topsoil 27
type 13
type and plant choices 135–36
sowing 167, 171, 178, 184
spotlighting 101
spread of plants 131
spring maintenance 167–71
steps
design considerations 73
how to build block and brick steps 74–79
maintenance 163
structure, planting 121
suckers, removing 174
summer maintenance 173–75
sump holes 105, 106

sunlight, garden aspect 14–15
sun-loving plants 134

T
time management 28–31
tools
  maintenance 162
  types and recommendations 38–41
topography 16–17
topsoil 27
trees
  feeding 184
  planting 142–44, 177
  pruning 168, 174, 183
  suggested choices 133
  ties and stakes 184
trellis 109

U
underwater lighting 101
upcycling 27

W
walls
  blockwork 82
  boundaries 47
  design considerations 81
  how to build a retaining wall 82–87
  maintenance 164
  materials 81
waste removal 19
water, drainage 14
water features
  design considerations 102–03
  how to build a sunken water feature 104–07
  maintenance 164, 170, 173, 180
watering 167, 173
weeding 167, 173, 177, 183
well-being 33
winter maintenance 183–85
wisteria 171, 174, 175, 184
wood chip, paths 53

Z
zonal lighting 101
zoning, historic 20

Acknowledgments

Author's acknowledgments

Writing a book has been one of the most rewarding accomplishments of my life, and with that, I'd like to take a moment to say a special thank you to my amazing team at DK: Lucy, Dawn, Barbara, Eleanor, and Ruth. Your attention to detail and unwavering support throughout this process has been exceptional, and this book simply wouldn't exist without your incredible contributions.

A big thank you as well to Clive Nichols for his stunning photography, capturing the garden through the seasons and braving the cold during our practical projects. Taking photos of cement mixers was definitely new territory for Clive, so I truly appreciate his adaptability and support every step of the way.

Another huge shout out to Chris Young, who believed in this book from the very beginning. Chris has supported my work over the years and played a major role in bringing this project to life.

To my wife, thank you for your patience, encouragement, and the flexibility that allowed me to pour everything I had into making this book a reality. Your support means everything.

I would like to dedicate this book to the thousands of young men who are no longer with us. This book gave me focus and drive during my own struggles with depression. Gardening has been my savior, and I want to honor those we've sadly lost to mental health battles, as well as those who are still on the journey of recovery. This book is for you.

And finally, to everyone who picks up this book and gives gardening a go, thank you! I hope it brings you the inspiration you need to tackle your own garden projects with confidence and joy.

Publisher's acknowledgments

DK would like to thank Clive Nichols for photography, Christo at Linework Render for illustrations, Adam Brackenbury for repro work, Kathryn Glendenning for the proofread, Ruth Ellis for the index, and John Tullock for US consulting.

Picture credits

The publisher would like to thank the following for their kind permission to reproduce their photographs:

(Key: a-above; b-below/bottom; c-center; f-far; l-left; r-right; t-top)

Henry Agg: 42, 49, 59t, 63tc, 63tr, 75t, 76tr, 76br, 77tr, 77cl, 77c, 78crb, 79tl, 83t, 85tl, 85tc, 86tl, 86cla, 106, 108, 113, 124;
Clive Nichols: 134, 134tl, 135tl, 135cla, 135clb, 135bl, 136tl, 136cla, 159

About the author

Henry Agg trained as a horticulturalist with the Royal Horticultural Society and in garden design at The English Gardening School. Before setting up his own garden design practice, Henry built a career on the corporate ladder, following his passion for gardening in his spare time. During that time, he established @henryagg on Instagram and shared how he transformed his garden while working full time and juggling family life. Now a qualified garden designer, Henry shares his design, landscaping, and planting knowledge. He passionately believes in the restorative benefits of gardening for mental well-being and proactively uses his platform to spread this message. Since becoming a garden designer, he has presented on *Gardeners' World* and *Alan Titchmarsh's Gardening Club*.

Editorial Director Ruth O'Rourke
Project Editor Lucy Philpott
Senior US Editor Megan Douglass
Gardening Design Manager Barbara Zuniga
Design Assistant Noor Ali
Senior Production Editor Tony Phipps
Senior Production Controller Samantha Cross
DTP and Design Coordinator Heather Blagden
Art Director Maxine Pedliham
Publishing Director Stephanie Jackson

Editorial Dawn Titmus
Jacket and layout design Eleanor Ridsdale
Photography Clive Nichols
Illustration Stuart Jackson-Carter

First American Edition, 2026
Published in the United States by DK Publishing,
a division of Penguin Random House LLC
1745 Broadway, 20th Floor, New York, NY 10019

26 27 28 29 30 10 9 8 7 6 5 4 3 2 1
001–345203–Feb/2026

ISBN: 979-8-2171-3374-1

Printed and bound in China

www.dk.com

This book was made with Forest Stewardship Council™ certified paper—one small step in DK's commitment to a sustainable future.
Learn more at www.dk.com/uk/information/sustainability